Reference citation for this volume:
Osborne, Richard; Calambokidis, J.; Dorsey, E.M., 1988.
  A guide to marine mammals of Greater Puget Sound.
  Anacortes, Wa.: Island Publishers.

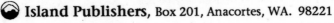 **Island Publishers**, Box 201, Anacortes, WA. 98221

Richard Osborne
John Calambokidis
and Eleanor M. Dorsey

with illustrations by
Albert Shepard and
Ed Newbold

A Guide to

Marine

 Island Publishers 1988

Mammals
of Greater Puget Sound

Produced under auspices of The Whale Museum, Friday Harbor, Washington

Book design and typography by Clifford Burke and Joseph Miller
using an Apple Macintosh II, Aldus' PageMaker and Stone types
from Adobe Systems. Maps and identifying silhouettes prepared
by Joseph Miller using Adobe's Illustrator. Output on a Linotronic
100. Registered trademarks all.

Printed in Hong Kong by Colour Communications of Seattle

Cover photo: Fred Felleman

Library of Congress Cataloging-in-Publication Data

Osborne, Richard, 1953-
  Marine mammals of greater Puget Sound.

  Bibliography: p.
  Includes index.
  1. Marine mammals--Washington (State)--Puget Sound Region--
Identification. 2. Mammals--Identification. 3. Mammals-- Wash-
ington (State)--Puget Sound Region--Identification. I. Calam-
bokidis, John, 1954- II. Dorsey, Eleanor M., 1948- . III. Title.
QH105.W2083 1987   599.5'09164'32 87-3414
ISBN 0-9615580-1-6

CONTENTS

ACKNOWLEDGEMENTS

Thanks are due to many people and institutions for the accomplishment of this book. We gratefully acknowledge the following: Delphine Haley and Thelma Palmer for being patient but persistent publishers with a good sense of humor, and a special mention for Delphine, whose editing helped synthesize the differing writing styles of three authors into one; Island Publishers and The Whale Museum for financing the project; Jim Cubbage for his early editorial review and assistance with the pinniped and mustelid accounts; Gretchen Steiger for assistance with the pinniped maps and species accounts; Jim Heimlich-Boran and Fred Felleman for assistance with the orca species account; Tim Ransom for review of the mustelid accounts; Mike Bigg for reviewing the orca identification drawings; Marilyn Dalheim, Steve Jeffries, Joe Scordino, Fred Felleman, Robin William Baird, Pam Stacy, Beth Miller, Debbie Miller, Rus Hoelzel and Mike Bigg for providing unpublished information; the Center for Coastal Studies, Provincetown, Massachusetts, and Okeanos Ocean Research Foundation, Hampton Bay, New York, for providing photographs; and the directors and staffs of Cascadia Research Collective and The Whale Museum for providing unpublished data and clerical support. Finally, we thank Ken Balcomb, Mike Bigg, Graeme Ellis, Bob Everitt, John Ford, Ian MacAskie, Gordon Pike, Victor Scheffer and John Slipp for their previously published field accounts on Pacific Northwest marine mammals.

FOREWORD

As a career zoologist living in the Pacific Northwest, I marvel at the rise of interest in local marine mammals during the past twenty years. It seems a fundamental sort of interest, and it is likely to endure. How did it arise? I suggest three reasons.

Improvements in zoological techniques—especially high speed photography, radiotelemetry, underwater sound recording and tissue analysis have begun to shed new light on sea mammal behavior and evolutionary relationships with other animals.

The dawning of the environmental age in the 1960s brought deeper appreciation of the values of wildlife forms, including sea mammals which had long been regarded as mere "resources" or had been killed when they interfered with commercial profit-taking. Witness the spread in popularity of whale watching and similar benign uses of wildlife.

The sheltered waters of the Pacific Northwest offer the best year-round sites anywhere in North America for studying or simply enjoying sea mammals in their natural habitats. This truth is not lost on the millions who visit these waters, nor on the owners of more than 200,000 pleasure boats registered in the State of Washington alone.

The book you are about to read is the distilled wisdom of three zoologists who have gone beyond scientific discovery: they have accepted the challenge of telling you in plain language what they have found. They aim to "enrich your experience of the inland waters." They ask you to share with them the pleasure of knowing about whales, dolphins, porpoises, seals, sea lions and otters. They suggest that you think about the implications of orca groups which mingle yet retain their separate dialects; about Dub-Dub, the seal who lived to a known age of thirty-three years; about California sea lions—unreported in Washington before 1954—which now appear in groups of up to a thousand; about man-made poisons in sea mammal tissues which attain, in Puget Sound, some of the highest levels recorded anywhere; and about gray whales that can swim 10,000 miles in the course of their yearly migration.

The authors hope that the book will foster "for generations to come" the preservation of the sea mammals of the Pacific Northwest. One does not hear a great deal about posterity these days. It is good to know that three zoologists, at least, are giving it thought.

> Victor B. Scheffer, Ph.D.
> Chairman (1973-1976)
> U.S. Marine Mammal Commission

10

ROBIN WILLIAM BAIRD

INTRODUCTION

The protected waters of Puget Sound, the San Juan Islands and southern Vancouver Island provide superb opportunities for observing marine mammals in the wild. Here, a great diversity of sea life thrives in the region's convoluted channels and protected bays, estuaries, beaches and fjords. Twice each day, this intricate network of marine waterways waxes and wanes with tidal exchanges up to 15 feet in height— movements which transform the waters into a "sea stew" of upwelling nutrients and organisms that course along powerful and varied currents to feed a vast number of marine communities. Blooms of plankton occur here throughout most of the year; these help support thousands of marine animals, including over twenty species of schooling fish. At the top of this food web, along with ourselves, is a group of warm-blooded, air-breathing, once land-living creatures that returned

11

to the sea—the marine mammals. Together we use a great variety of the food species available here throughout the year.

After the recession of glaciers from the Greater Puget Sound basin some 8,000 years ago, the first humans and marine mammals arrived to enjoy centuries of mutual subsistence on the natural abundance of the region. To many native peoples, marine mammals were regarded as supernatural guides or as indicators of fishing conditions. Orcas, seals and sea lions adorned their totem poles as clan spirits, incorporating these animals' talents as intelligent and successful hunters into family lineages. Many myths reflect a reverence for certain marine mammals as recipients of supernatural forces. Orcas or killer whales, for instance, were of major symbolic importance, even among tribes of diverse origins. Several legends describe them as humans that had been banished into the sea, and it was always considered bad luck to kill one.

Those native groups that subsisted heavily on marine mammals—the Nootka of Vancouver Island and the Makah of the Olympic Peninsula—also held the orca and several other marine mammals as important totems. The Nootka and the Makah obtained a substantial amount of their food, clothing and tools from seals, humpback whales and gray whales, using methods not found in neighboring groups. However, even in the case of the Nootka and Makah, hunting probably did not noticeably affect the abundance of any marine mammal species during these early times.

The story of white settlement in the region was not so pleasant for marine mammals. They were immediately exploited heavily for skins, oil and meat. The great whales were hunted to near extinction both by commercial whalers and "gun-happy" locals. Seals were

12

greatly depleted, and sea otters nearly became extinct. Later came conflicts and competition with commercial fishermen; destruction of habitat and food sources through logging, hydroelectric dams and shoreline development; and decades of pollution. In spite of these impacts, today we still see thriving populations of marine mammals, some of which are recovering to previous levels of abundance as a result of our efforts to change some of the irresponsible practices of the recent past. Nonetheless, other species, such as the northern right whale, continue to hover near the brink of extinction.

Three distinct types of marine mammals occur in Greater Puget Sound—cetaceans, pinnipeds and mustelids. Cetaceans—the whales, dolphins and porpoises—have evolved to spend their lives totally in the sea. Pinnipeds—the seals, sea lions and walrus—hunt and feed exclusively in the ocean but come ashore to rest, to mate and to bear and nurse their young. Although most mustelids—the otters, weasels, skunks and wolverines—are terrestrial, some otters regularly swim and feed in the ocean, giving them status as marine mammals in this book.

In the pages that follow, we describe the identification marks, natural history and local distribution of the wild marine mammals that have been documented in Greater Puget Sound. Each species is labeled as common, occasional, rare, or accidental, with the rarest presented together at the end of each major section. For two common species of cetaceans—the resident orcas (killer whales) and the minke whales—we provide identification drawings and brief biographies of all the known individuals. Quick references for identifying common marine mammals are found on the inside covers. Also included are a formal taxonomic

13

listing of all species involved, procedures for reporting marine mammal strandings, tips on how to observe the more common species and a summary of marine mammal conservation.

Equipped with this information, we hope you will be prepared to identify any marine mammal, common or rare, that occurs in Greater Puget Sound. In the case of orcas and minkes, you may even be able to recognize the individual whale and learn his or her name– along with some interesting particulars about that whale. All of this is provided with the hope that it will enrich your experience of the inland waters and help ensure the preservation of this region's marine mammals for generations to come.

Cetaceans

Cetaceans—the whales, dolphins and porpoises—are those mammals that eons ago left the land in favor of spending their lives totally in water. The name of their

15

taxonomic order, Cetacea, is derived from the Greek word *ketos* and the Latin word *cetus*, both meaning whale. There are two living subdivisions: the Odontoceti, or toothed whales; and the Mysticeti, or baleen whales. Like other placental mammals, cetaceans are warm-blooded and give birth to live young which are nursed with mammary glands. However, unlike other mammals, the cetaceans have lost their hind legs entirely and are totally aquatic and unable to travel on land. Except for a few facial hairs in some species, cetaceans have replaced all of the characteristic mammalian fur and hair on their bodies with an elastic skin and a thick layer of fatty blubber. Their shape has become streamlined to aid in movement through water: the nostrils have migrated to the top of the head to facilitate breathing; the forelimbs have become flippers; and the hindquarters have developed into giant paddles known as tail flukes, which propel the body through the water by powerful up and down undulations. With over 65 million years of evolution behind them, the once-terrestrial cetaceans have fully adapted to their aquatic habitat.

TOOTHED WHALES

Suborder Odontoceti

Toothed whales or odontocetes include six families and up to eighty species worldwide, ranging in size from the relatively small dolphins and porpoises, to narwhals, beaked whales, killer whales (orcas) and the giant sperm whales—like the legendary Moby Dick. All odontocetes have a single blowhole and at least two teeth. Probably all use echolocation clicks to navigate underwater and

17

locate prey. Most odontocetes also produce high-frequency whistles which are believed to be used for social communication. Beyond these similarities, however, they are an extremely diverse group.

Species from four families of the toothed whales are found in Greater Puget Sound. Described in the following pages, they are two porpoise species from the family Phocoenidae; seven dolphins from the large and diverse family Delphinidae; three or four beaked whales from the little known family Ziphiidae; and one representative from the sperm whales of the family Physeteridae.

BETH MILLER

DALL'S PORPOISE
Phocoenoides dalli

Having been tracked at 30 knots, Dall's porpoises are the fastest cetaceans of the inland waters. They are the most likely species to be riding your vessel's bow wave in Greater Puget Sound, and, although they are small and black and white, they are not "a herd of baby killer whales," as is so often reported to the Whale Museum's Whale Hotline. Known as "broken tail" to both the Quillayutes and the Makahs, probably because of a characteristic kink in the tailstock, the Dall's porpoise is today the most common cetacean in northern Puget Sound and the Strait of Juan de Fuca.

IDENTIFICATION Small and chunky with tiny flippers and tail flukes, the Dall's porpoise is not too difficult to identify, especially when it races along displaying its characteristic "rooster tail" splash. It is boldly marked—black overall with a large white patch on the flanks and belly and varying amounts of white at the tip of the dorsal fin and along the trailing edge of the tail

19

flukes. The head, lacking a noticeable beak, is small, as is the triangular dorsal fin. The tailstock has a small kink or bump about half-way between the dorsal fin and the tail flukes. Newborn Dall's porpoises are 3 or 4 feet in length, and adults can attain just over 6 1/2 feet.

When the Dall's porpoise swims slowly and rolls at the surface, it is often mistaken for its smaller gray-brown cousin, the harbor porpoise. From a distance, the two species are almost impossible to distinguish. Look closely for their color, or, when that is not possible (often due to silhouetting), look for the kink in the tailstock and note carefully the shape of the dorsal fin.

A bow-riding Dall's porpoise shows its stocky body, white flank patch, and white fluke and dorsal fin markings.   JAMES T. HARVEY

The dorsal fin of the Dall's porpoise has a longer following edge than leading edge; the harbor porpoise is just the opposite, having a longer leading edge.

NATURAL HISTORY Dall's porpoises occur throughout the temperate waters of the North Pacific from Japan and southern California to as far north as the

20

Bering Sea. They feed primarily on squid and small schooling fishes, with generalized movements north in the spring and south in the fall. In the open ocean, they usually occur in schools numbering in the hundreds; along the continental shelf and in the inland waters, they form smaller groups of between two and fifteen individuals. Probably in response to a seasonal abundance of prey, groups of up to sixty individuals are sometimes seen during spring in Haro Strait and the Strait of Juan de Fuca. Calves are born in summer, and gestation is thought to be about one year.

The 1986 population estimate for Dall's porpoises in the North Pacific was 920,000—a high figure that incorrectly suggests a secure population. Dall's porpoises in the Gulf of Alaska are currently under heavy pressure from the Japanese drift net fishery, which entangles and drowns an estimated 5,000 to 10,000 of these cetaceans annually. Analysis of a sample of these entangled animals has revealed that as many as eighty percent of these dead Dall's porpoises are pregnant and/or nursing females. This suggests that the region is an important nursery area and that the entanglements may have a higher impact on the population than simple numbers would suggest. Recent rulings in the United States federal courts will attempt to bring the kill down to fewer than 2,000 per year, beginning in 1987. Off Vancouver Island's outer coast, Japanese drift net fishing was tested in 1986 and 1987, resulting in significant numbers of marine bird and mammal kills. Because of this, British Columbia has decided not to open up the fishery to the Japanese in the future. In Greater Puget Sound, the small salmon gill nets used by local fishermen are responsible for some entanglement of porpoises, but the level of impact is unknown.

Researchers studying Dall's porpoises in Greater

Puget Sound are using photographs to identify individuals from the white pigmentation patterns on the dorsal fin and tail flukes and by major nicks and scars on the body. Most of this research is being conducted in the waters along the south end of Whidbey Island and in the vicinity of Haro Strait. Preliminary results from research in the Whidbey Island area suggest that Dall's porpoises are present all year long, with mating and calving taking place in the inland waters.

LOCAL DISTRIBUTION In the inland waters, Dall's porpoises are common north of Seattle throughout the year. In recent years, they are also being sighted more often in the southern reaches of Puget Sound. The most reliable viewing sites are in Admiralty Inlet and Saratoga Passage along the south end of Whidbey Island, in Haro Strait along the United States-Canadian border and throughout the Strait of Juan de Fuca.

HOW TO OBSERVE Similar in behavior to white-sided dolphins, Dall's porpoises are enthusiastic bow riders, often finding the observers, rather than the other way

*Dall's Porpoise
Distribution*

22

With its characteristic "rooster tail" splash, the Dall's porpoise can attain speeds up to 30 knots. FRED FELLEMAN

around. However, unlike white-sided dolphins, they can be spotted easily from boats when they are engaged in activities other than bow riding, and they can also be seen from many places on shore.

When you are at sea in a moving boat and encounter these cetaceans, continue past them in a straight line at about 5 knots. They may choose to ride the bow wave. If so, keep the boat at a steady speed and course. Do not turn sharply! If they do not ride the bow wave, they may be feeding or traveling in the opposite direction. If they are traveling in the opposite direction, try moving along (100 yards away) in the direction in which they are heading and they may hitch a ride on your bow wave. If they are feeding, stop the boat 100 yards away and just watch as they roll slowly at the surface. When feeding, they tend to stay in one general region; if you drift quietly with your motor off, they may mill around your

23

boat. When drifting with feeding Dall's porpoises, do not start your boat up again until they have moved 100 yards away.

From shore, Dall's porpoises are most easily observed from Limekiln Whale Watch Park on San Juan Island or anywhere along the west and south sides of Whidbey Island.

FRED FELLEMAN

HARBOR PORPOISE
Phocoena phocoena

One of the most abundant cetaceans in Puget Sound four decades ago, the harbor porpoise was reportedly common enough to be seen on any day of the year throughout the inland waters of Washington State. Today, however, it appears only occasionally in Puget Sound proper, occurring primarily in the northern reaches around the San Juan Islands and the Strait of Juan de Fuca. This is a shy, retiring animal that may not be able to tolerate the increasing presence of humans on the inland waters.

IDENTIFICATION The harbor porpoise is recognized by its small overall size, small triangular dorsal fin and brownish color. Just under 3 feet at birth, it reaches only 6 feet at maturity. It is gray-brown to black on top, with lighter gray on the undersides that extends along the flanks, turning almost white on the belly. The flukes, flippers and the small dorsal fin are all dark brown-gray.

25

The triangular dorsal fin has a longer leading edge than following edge.

Harbor porpoises usually travel singly or in groups of two to six, and it is sometimes difficult to distinguish them from flotsam bobbing on the surface. They are often mistaken for Dall's porpoises, but they may be distinguished by dorsal fin shape, coloration and behavior. The harbor porpoise has a dorsal fin that is shaped in reverse from that of the Dall's porpoise, i.e., with a longer leading edge than following edge. The solid gray-brown harbor porpoise is very quiet and shy around boats. It never bow rides and seems to avoid vessel traffic. Although this cetacean has been known to breach out of the water on rare occasions, it is not usually very splashy, surfacing instead in slow rolls. In contrast, the stark black and white Dall's porpoise tends to approach boats to bow ride and creates a "rooster tail" splash when it swims fast.

NATURAL HISTORY   Harbor porpoises occur in coastal regions of both the North Atlantic and North

Harbor Porpoise Distribution

26

Pacific, from the subarctic south to temperate zones. They feed on squid, shrimp and small schooling fish, such as herring and candlefish. Gestation is believed to be around eleven months, with calving in late spring and early summer. Sexual maturity is estimated at four years of age. During summer and early fall, larger aggregations of fifty or more are seen, possibly in relation to mating activity. Their lifespan is relatively short for a cetacean—probably not exceeding fifteen or twenty years.

Because of their nearshore and coastal habits, harbor porpoises are in close contact with human activities that increasingly threaten them. In many regions, including local waters, these marine mammals are known to carry some of the highest levels of contamination found in cetaceans. Harbor propoises also become entangled and drown in many types of fishing gear, and they are disturbed by concentrated vessel activity. In local waters, all of these factors may be contributing to the decline in their numbers in some areas.

LOCAL DISTRIBUTION Harbor porpoises still occur throughout Greater Puget Sound but are rare south of the San Juan Islands and the Strait of Juan de Fuca. Although they can be found during any month of the year, the largest concentrations are found in summer and early fall in the northern San Juan Islands, where groups of more than sixty individuals have been seen.

HOW TO OBSERVE When you encounter these shy mammals at sea, maintain the same speed and course and simply watch them as you pass by. Never try to follow harbor porpoises or change speed or course when near them because they will be scared away. In fact, it is best to observe them from shore or from a silent boat, such as a kayak or sailboat. Under these conditions, the porpoises may not notice you and may approach closely on their own. They will disappear quickly at the sound of a running engine.

From shore, harbor porpoises are most easily seen from Limekiln Whale Watch Park on San Juan Island and Washington Park on Fidalgo Island near the Anacortes ferry dock.

FRED FELLEMAN

ORCA
Orcinus orca

The orca—also commonly called killer whale—is the most dramatic and best known cetacean in Greater Puget Sound. We are fortunate to have within this natural "aquarium" a resident orca population whose members we can recognize and encounter over and over again. Aided by a photographic identification technique which Canadian biologist Michael Bigg developed in 1973, we have acquired an intimate view into the life history and behavior of local orca individuals and their pods. This joint research by field scientists in

29

both Canada and the United States has resulted in one of the longest and most thorough studies of wild cetaceans ever conducted.

IDENTIFICATION The orca, largest member of the dolphin family, is easily identified by its fairly large size, distinctive white-on-black markings and large dorsal fin—particularly on adult males. The flippers are paddle-shaped and also very large—again noticeably larger on adult males. The white markings consist of a small oval patch just behind the eye and a large area covering most of the undersides, including all of the lower jaw and throat and part of the flanks. There is also a whitish-gray saddle patch behind the dorsal fin. These white and gray patches tend to vary in shape and intensity among populations, as well as between individuals. The variation in the saddle patch, along with the size, shape and markings of the dorsal fin, have been used by field researchers as the basis for long-term identification of individuals from photographs.

Orcas range in length from 8 feet at birth to about 30 feet as adult males and 24 feet as adult females. The prominent black dorsal fin grows to almost 3 feet in height in females and up to 6 feet in males. The smaller fin of females and young is also more curved than in adult bulls. A useful fact to remember is that if the height of an orca's fin is greater than the width of the fin at its base, then this animal is sure to be an adult male. Therefore, any orca with a dorsal fin that is not noticeably taller than it is wide at the base is either an adult female or a juvenile.

Orcas usually travel in groups of between five and twenty, but groups of over 100 individuals have also been recorded. Occasionally they are found alone; these are almost always adult bulls. The very rare lone female could be mistaken for a minke whale from a distance

Orca fins vary according to sex and age. This adult bull's fin towers above the female and calf fins in the foreground.   A. RUS HOELZEL

because of her small hooked fin, but the fin of a minke whale is located much farther back on the body.

In general, the tall straight fin of the male and the white markings make orcas unmistakable. However, when adult males are not present, orcas might be confused with pilot whales, Risso's dolphins or false killer whales. When making an identification, remember that all of these species are significantly smaller than orcas and lack bright white patches. Risso's dolphins can be distinguished by the increasing amount of white around the head in adults and noticeable white tooth-rakes all over the body. False killer whales and pilot whales have more bulbous heads and stubbier dorsal

31

fins than the orca, particularly the pilot whale. Groups of black and white Dall's porpoises are sometimes reported as a "herd of baby orcas." However, only newborn orcas are as small as porpoises, and they would never travel unaccompanied by adults.

NATURAL HISTORY With a powerfully muscled body that can attain speeds up to 25 knots, orcas are the sea's top predators. They are found throughout the world but are generally more concentrated at higher latitudes and in areas of high biological productivity. In many places, the seasonal occurrence of orcas has been correlated with the presence of a particular kind of prey: southern

A young resident orca plays with a salmon before eating it.

KEN BALCOMB

elephant seals and penguins in the south Indian Ocean; northern elephant seals in California; sea lions in Oregon and Argentina; herring in the northeast Atlantic and salmon in the eastern North Pacific.

Although they are famous for preying on other marine mammals, orcas actually feed on a diversity of prey, ranging from the largest baleen whales and all sizes of toothed whales (including sperm whales and other orcas) to seals and sea lions, numerous types of fish, sea turtles, birds, squid and octopus. Because of this varied taste, orcas have been called generalized and opportunistic feeders, but closer examination suggests that they actually specialize on a prey abundant in their particular

With its penis erect, a young male orca courts a potential partner.
BARBARA TODD

area and probably shift their prey preferences in response to seasonal changes. This type of feeding strategy is shared with the most efficient of the terrestrial carnivores, including hunting and gathering humans. Most detailed accounts of orca feeding behavior describe hunting as a coordinated group, similar to group hunting in wolves, hyenas, lions and humans.

The age of sexual maturity in orcas is not precisely known. Dorsal fin growth is noticeable in males between the ages of twelve and thirteen, but they do not reach full size until their late teens or early twenties. For females, first births in captivity suggest that they mature sexually at around nine or ten years of age, while in the wild females give birth to their first calf between the ages of thirteen and seventeen.

There does not appear to be any specific breeding

33

season for orcas, although most mating behavior in Puget Sound is seen during summer and fall when the three resident pods join together into multi-pod groups to feed cooperatively on migrating salmon. Pregnant cows give birth after about sixteen months' gestation, and births have been documented throughout the year. The shortest interval observed between calves for orcas in Washington and British Columbia is three years, although the average calving rate for females in these waters is closer to once every eight years. In general, orcas are slow reproducers but they are very long-lived, surviving at least into their forties or fifties and perhaps several decades longer.

Orca calves are 7 1/2 to 8 feet in length at birth and are probably always assisted into the world by at least one other whale in addition to its mother. The newborn is recognized by its extremely small size and its proximity to either its mother, grandmother or adolescent sister. Small calves always surface in the immediate wake of their mother or babysitter because in this position they get help swimming from the suction of the larger whale's body as it moves through the water. Another distinguishing feature of very young calves is a peachy tinge to its white spots which some researchers believe is caused by jaundice—the result of an immature liver not removing bile quickly enough from the circulatory system.

The orca's infancy lasts for about the first two years. During the first six months, it practically never leaves its mother's side. After this period, it ventures short distances to investigate other whales and is more likely to be entrusted for babysitting to an immediate relative. How long orcas nurse is unknown, but it is safe to conclude that they do so at least for the first six months and possible that they continue into the third year.

A young calf hitches a free ride at its mother's side in the "echelon position." JAMES HEIMLICH-BORAN

The juvenile stage for orcas lasts from about two to six or even eight years of age and is characterized by increasing independence, although nearly always the young whale is in the proximity of its mother and/or immediate relatives. Like most young mammals, curiosity and active play with peers are the major activities of this age. Quite often, chasing and splashing groups of juveniles are seen either on their own or under the supervision of only one adult whale. Sometimes the adult supervisor is a mature bull, with no adult females anywhere in the immediate vicinity.

As adolescents, orcas act more like adults, although they are noticeably smaller in physical appearance. This stage begins at around seven years and ends at thirteen to seventeen years of age in females and fifteen to nineteen in males. Adolescence is characterized by less

35

play, with the females spending more time apparently caring for younger whales and the adolescent males sometimes on their own or hanging around the bulls.

Orcas in Washington and British Columbia waters can be divided into three distinct pod communities that have separate call dialects, or "languages," different feeding strategies and noticeably different social behaviors. These three large pod groupings are referred to as the northern resident community (13 pods of approximately 170 whales), the southern resident community (3 pods of approximately 80 whales) and the transient community (17 pods of approximately 50 whales). The two resident communities have separate ranges that do not overlap and seem to be defined by the tidal boundary half-way up the east side of Vancouver Island at the north end of Georgia Strait between Powell and Comox Rivers. The transient community travels throughout the range of both resident communities and beyond. From the few times that actual mating has been observed in these orcas, it appears that breeding occurs between individuals from different pods but within the same community. Thus, these three pod communities have probably been socially and reproductively isolated for many generations.

Ongoing studies in Greater Puget Sound are revealing differences between the behavior and ecology of the southern resident community and the seven local pods of the transient community. Residents and transients feed differently and are different in appearance; they travel in different-sized family groups and exhibit community-specific genetic differences in their chromosomes. The resident orcas have more rounded dorsal fins and more variable saddle patches. They occur in large groups of five to thirty individuals of both sexes and all ages, and, on many occasions in summer and fall, they converge into multi-pod groupings of up to eighty whales. Transient pods, on the other hand, are much smaller, having only one to five members. Although they will sometimes join together into temporary multi-pod groups, transient gatherings are smaller, usually including only up to ten individuals. Unlike the resident pods which feed mainly on fish, transients consume other marine mammals, and in Greater Puget Sound they are most often seen preying on harbor seals.

A well-known orca family, L-Pod, cruises Haro Strait off San Juan Island. FRED FELLEMAN

Resident whales have rarely been known to eat marine mammals, and they are often seen near seals, sea lions or other whales with no predatory reaction.

Each of the three pod communities produces different calls; each breeds and socially interacts only within itself; and each has its own travel routes, feeding strategies and social behaviors. In general, the two resident communities are more similar to each other than to the transient community. This may be due to similarities in prey and closer historical and genetic relationships.

37

The two resident communities sometimes show significant differences in social behavior, however. For example, the "greeting ceremony" and the "intermingling ceremony" are two behaviors enacted only by the orcas of the southern resident community—J, K and L-Pods, the eighty-three orcas featured in the Guide to Individual Orcas on page 147. Almost always, when any of these pods reunite after a separation of a day or more, they engage in a greeting ceremony in which the two pods line up abreast, hover at the surface facing each other and then swim into each other. The greeting ceremony is usually followed by intermingling. This is a behavior in which whales from the different pods break off into tight swarms and rub and roll around on each other, individually coming in contact with each whale from the other pod. Intermingling also occurs when pods awaken after a multi-pod sleeping session.

Since mating, like most orca behavior, takes place primarily underwater, scientists have not been able to determine any of the fathers of the thirty-two calves that have been documented for the southern resident community to date. But, by following the long-term relationships between mothers, calves and siblings and by noting the frequencies with which they associate at the surface, a great deal has been learned about other aspects of this community's social organization. Within each pod, certain groups of individuals are consistently found together during most activities. Scientists believe that these consistent "subgroups" within the pods are actually family units consisting of mothers and their offspring. They have observed that no whale has ever been seen to leave its mother's subgroup, nor has any whale joined a subgroup other than through birth. Of the twenty-four whales that have disappeared in the southern resident community since the photo-identification study began, none has reappeared in any of the other pods between Puget Sound and Prince William Sound, Alaska. Therefore, it appears that no individuals, not even the huge bulls, ever leave their mother's subgroup. Thus, if a whale disappears from its pod, it must be presumed dead. This type of social organization—in which both males and females spend their entire lives with their mothers—has never been observed in another species, terrestrial or aquatic, and may be unique to orcas, perhaps even unique to these resident pods. Whether the transient pods in Greater Puget Sound or orcas in other regions of the world also have this unusual social organization is not yet known.

LOCAL DISTRIBUTION Orcas travel as much as 100 miles every twenty-four hours, swimming continuously throughout the day and night. The southern resident pods (J, K, and L-Pods) stay within a radius of about 200 miles of the San Juan Islands year-round. Their movements appear to be dictated by the distribution of salmon. The transient pods range much farther—north

Orca Distribution

39

all the way to southern Alaska and perhaps as far south as Oregon or even California. The seven transient pods in Greater Puget Sound have somewhat unpredictable movements that appear attuned more to preying on harbor seals and bottom fish than on salmon.

"Kelping" is a favorite orca pastime. The kelp is often rubbed across the body or used in play. LINDA CAMPBELL

The resident orcas of Greater Puget Sound follow the primary routes of resident and migrating salmon. When salmon fishing is good in any one area, it is likely that orcas will appear within a few days to feed on them, unless the salmon are more abundant in some other part of their home range. The orcas in J-Pod usually cruise the inland waters east of Race Rocks in the Strait of Juan de Fuca. K-Pod and L-Pod, on the other hand, regularly travel out the Strait of Juan de Fuca and along the outer coast. From late May through October, however, all three pods are most often found feeding on migrating salmon between the eastern Strait of Juan de

Fuca and the mouth of the Fraser River. This is a good time of year for orca watching in the Gulf Islands and the San Juan Islands, particularly along Haro Strait. During summer and fall, orcas also frequent Admiralty Inlet and Puget Sound proper, traveling along the southeast side of Whidbey Island, south past Seattle and Bainbridge Island, along either side of Vashon Island and on through the Tacoma Narrows as far as the Nisqually Delta.

As mentioned above, the movements of transient pods are essentially unpredictable. They can show up almost anywhere, even in shallow estuaries and dead-end bays and at any time of the year. While residents are never in one area for more than a couple of hours,

A "spyhopping" orca scans the horizon. FRED FELLEMAN 41

transients will sometimes spend up to a week in a given region.

HOW TO OBSERVE   When encountering orcas, whether they be resident or transient, observe the established guidelines. These are guidelines that have been established for all marine mammals by the National Marine Fisheries Service in accordance with the United States Marine Mammal Protection Act of 1972. Move slowly and approach the whales from the side, traveling parallel to them at the same speed as the slowest animals. Vessels should not approach closer than 100 yards and should never separate mothers and offspring. Aircraft should not fly lower than 1000 feet. In general, you should not perform any action that disrupts normal behavior.

However, if the whales should decide to approach closely, it is not a violation if your boat is not moving or if it is traveling on a straight course parallel or away from them—as long as the boat either remains stationary or moves back outside the 100-yard limit. Any boat that is repeatedly too close to the whales is in violation of the federal guidelines.

Researchers studying the whales must have special permits issued by the National Marine Fisheries Service that allow them to approach closer. These vessels are marked as research vessels and fly a yellow flag with a permit number on it. All other vessels must follow the whale-watching guidelines above.

To observe orcas from shore, Limekiln Whale Watch Park on the west side of San Juan Island is the best site between June and September. Other areas along the major routes of the whales are less predictable. To observe orcas from a wildlife cruise boat, contact The Whale Museum in Friday Harbor for current schedules throughout the region.

MICHAEL NEWCOMER

PACIFIC WHITE-SIDED DOLPHIN

Lagenorhynchus obliquidens

Along with bottlenose dolphins, belugas and orcas, white-sided dolphins are the most common cetaceans displayed in zoos and aquariums. Sometimes called "Lags" after their scientific name, white-sided dolphins are classic coastal-to-oceanic dolphins. They love to ride the bow of both large and small vessels and to leap from the water, and they can often be found traveling with

43

other species of small cetaceans. There are six species within the genus Lagenorhynchus, with representatives in every ocean of the world, except in the high arctic north of the Bering Sea.

IDENTIFICATION The Pacific white-sided dolphin may be recognized from a distance by its relatively small size—3 feet at birth to 8 feet at maturity—and a large curved dorsal fin that often displays light shading along the trailing edge. At closer range, a distinctive color pattern is also visible on the body, especially when these dolphins leap out of the water. They are grayish-black above with noticeably pale sides and a white belly. One or two pale gray stripes, sometimes called suspenders, extend along the dark back from the head to the tailstock. The beak is short and dark and, as a result, inconspicuous.

The white-sided dolphin's very prominent, strongly curved dorsal fin should prevent confusion with harbor porpoises and Dall's porpoises, both of which have small triangular fins. This dolphin is also larger, surfaces higher in the water than either the Dall's or harbor porpoise and does not produce the Dall's porpoise's characteristic rooster tail splash when swimming fast.

Occasionally, in more southerly waters, white-sided dolphins may be mistaken for saddleback dolphins with which they regularly associate, but saddleback dolphins have long noticeable beaks and the dark color on their backs forms a characteristic V-shaped saddle.

Although they are considerably smaller, white-sided dolphins might also be confused at first sight with Risso's dolphins, false killer whales, pilot whales or even orcas. In contrast, Risso's dolphins are uniform gray, blending to white near the head, and also have more pointed dorsal fins. False killer whales are completely dark, with more pointed dorsal fins than white-sided dolphins. Pilot whales have prominent, bulbous heads and are dark in color, except for a faint gray saddle; they also have dorsal fins that have a wider base and are set farther forward than in the white-sided dolphin. The orca's large size, taller and straighter fin and its stark black and white color should clearly distinguish it from the white-sided dolphin.

NATURAL HISTORY White-sided dolphins travel in groups of between fifty and several hundred individuals; however, in coastal waters they are usually seen in smaller groups of five to fifteen. They feed on squid and small fish and are most common in our waters during summer and fall, which appears to be their major breeding and calving season. Calves are born after twelve months' gestation, and sexual maturity is estimated at between six and ten years of age. They move north in spring and south in fall, ranging from the Gulf of Alaska in summer to Baja California in winter. They are avid bow riders and acrobats, often sighted from considerable distances due to their breaching and

*Pacific White-Sided
Dolphin Distribution*

45

splashing. Current population estimates for white-sided dolphins in the North Pacific range between 30,000 and 50,000 individuals.

LOCAL DISTRIBUTION   White-sided dolphins are regular summer and fall inhabitants of the Strait of Juan de Fuca, particularly around Race Rocks on Vancouver Island. Occasionally small groups are seen in Haro Strait off San Juan Island. Farther into the inland waters, usually only pairs or lone individuals are sighted. Some of these loners have been reported jumping and frolicking near divers and boats; more often, they are found wandering aimlessly, eventually stranding on a beach. In recent years, a white-sided dolphin stranded alive in southern Puget Sound and was held for rehabilitation at Point Defiance Aquarium in Tacoma. Unfortunately, it succumbed to the conditions that had probably stranded it in the first place.

HOW TO OBSERVE   White-sided dolphins often approach vessels to ride the bow wave. When this happens, the vessel should just continue its course, maintain the same speed and enjoy the show. Do not slow down rapidly or change course radically. If you see a group of white-sided dolphins and they don't approach to bow ride, then stay 100 yards away or shut down and drift, because they may be feeding or sick or injured. Being primarily an outer-coast or open-ocean species, white-sided dolphins would probably not be sighted from shore anywhere in Greater Puget Sound.

ROBERT PITMAN

NORTHERN RIGHT WHALE DOLPHIN
Lissodelphis borealis

Although the northern right whale dolphin has never been officially documented in the inland waters, one unconfirmed report of a group of five was made in 1977 in Puget Sound. These dolphins are occasional bow riders and relatively common off the Washington coast. Often they travel with white-sided dolphins, pilot whales and Risso's dolphins.

IDENTIFICATION Northern right whale dolphins are readily identifiable because they lack a dorsal fin and are

47

mostly black, except for a white belly patch that is widest at the pectoral flippers. Occasionally on the lower jaw there is a small white patch that extends slightly beyond the upper jaw. Newborns are lighter in color than adults and just over 2 feet in length. Adults reach a maximum length of 10 feet. These slim-bodied dolphins are most common off the coast from April to October. They will probably not be confused with any other cetacean—although they could be mistaken for a herd of fast-swimming sea lions from a distance.

MICHAEL NEWCOMER

SADDLEBACK DOLPHIN
Delphinus delphis

The saddleback dolphin, also known as the common dolphin, is rare north of the California-Oregon border. Its only recorded appearance in the inland waters was a stranding in April 1953 off Victoria, British Columbia.

IDENTIFICATION Saddleback dolphins are oceanic cetaceans rarely found in coastal waters or in groups fewer than 100. In the open ocean, they form herds sometimes in excess of 2,000. The dorsal fin is prominent and slightly curved, and the pectoral flippers are long and thin. These dolphins are black on their backs from the prominent beak to the middle of the tailstock; this black coloration extends farther down the sides, just under the dorsal fin, forming a dark V-shaped

49

SADDLE BACK DOLPHIN

saddle on the back—hence the species' name. The sides are tan or gray from the eye to the tail, and the belly is white. The black dorsal fin often has a gray area in the middle. Saddleback dolphins are slightly under 3 feet at birth and reach a maximum of about 8 feet in adult males. The only locally-occurring species with which this dolphin might be mistaken is the Pacific white-sided dolphin, which is the same size and has a similarly prominent dorsal fin. The white-sided dolphin is distin-quished by two thin pale stripes through its dark shoul-der and back, a more strongly curved dorsal fin with a pale color extending to the rear margin, and a beak that is barely noticeable.

50

LARRY HOBBS

RISSO'S DOLPHIN
Grampus griseus

Risso's dolphin, also known as the whitehead grampus, is common off the Washington coast, but it usually prefers deeper waters where it can feed predominantly on squid. The only records of this species in the inland waters are two strandings, one in Discovery Bay in the eastern Strait of Juan de Fuca in March of 1975 and another near Port Angeles in October of 1987.

IDENTIFICATION The Risso's dolphin is approximately 5 feet in length at birth and 14 feet at maturity. The adult is distinguished by a large (15-inch), curved dorsal fin and a large, almost square, forehead or melon.

51

A dark indentation runs vertically from the middle of the forehead almost to the mouth, but it is rarely visible at sea. These cetaceans are dark gray in color when young, with lighter gray on the undersides. As they mature, they acquire many pale scars around the head and fewer scars farther back on the body. Eventually the scarring turns the adult's head white and much of the rest of the body pale gray. The pectoral flippers and flukes are long and slender. Risso's dolphins occur in groups of five to over one hundred and are often found in the company of right whale dolphins and pilot whales. Although these cetaceans are usually fairly distinct because of their pale coloration as adults, they could be confused from a distance with pilot whales, false killer whales or, possibly, orcas. Pilot whales have shorter, more widely-based dorsal fins; false killer whales are glossy black in color; and orcas are black and white, with very tall dorsal fins in adult males. Look for the Risso's dolphin's scarring and lighter coloration to distinguish it from these other species.

SUSAN SHANE

SHORT-FINNED PILOT WHALE

Globicephala macrorhynchus

Pilot whales have historically been known to coastal natives of the Pacific Northwest. The Quillayutes of the Olympic coast called them "mole whales," probably because their bulbous heads tend to plow through the water as they surface for air. Fishermen have called them "pilot whales" in the belief that these animals would lead them to their catch. Today they are only occasionally reported on the coasts of Washington and southern

53

Vancouver Island, usually when a fisherman describes an animal that would be difficult to identify as anything else but a pilot whale. Although primarily an oceanic and continental shelf species, these small whales occasionally wander into the Strait of Juan de Fuca and into the inland waters during summer and fall, possibly when following squid—their preferred prey.

IDENTIFICATION   Traits that distinguish the pilot whale include a prominent bulbous forehead that tends to plow through the water when surfacing and a low curved dorsal fin with an unusually wide base that is relatively close to the blowhole. Ranging in length from about 5 feet at birth to 14 feet in adult females and 18 feet in adult males, this small whale is slate-gray to black, with lighter gray markings on the undersides and a faded gray saddle patch similar to that of the orca, but less noticeable and less distinct.

In the inland and coastal waters, pilot whales usually travel in groups of five to ten but congregate in larger groups of more than 100 in the open ocean. Of the whales and dolphins likely to be encountered in this region, only the false killer whale—which is essentially the same size as the pilot whale and travels in similar-sized groups—should pose problems in identification for the experienced observer. However, the novice may also confuse pilot whales with orcas or dolphins, as a result of a brief or distant encounter. All of these animals have dorsal fins that are taller, narrower at the base and placed farther back toward the middle of the body; none has a forehead as bulbous as the pilot whale's. To distinguish further, dolphins are noticeably smaller; orcas have bright white patches; and false killer whales are completely black on top with no gray saddle behind the dorsal fin.

Recent evidence suggests that female pilot whales can

A pilot whale launches skyward, showing its long sickle-shaped pectoral fin and lightly colored saddle area. SUSAN SHANE

55

still reproduce at the age of forty years and may be able to continue nursing into their mid-fifties, with calves not being weaned until five to seven years of age. If so, even grandmothers would be capable of sharing nursing duties. This suggests that maternal lineages may be important in the pilot whale's social organization, as appears to be the case for orcas. No specific season for mating and calving has been delineated, but gestation is estimated at about fifteen months.

JOHN CALAMBOKIDIS

FALSE KILLER WHALE

Pseudorca crassidens

The false killer whale is an oceanic species normally not found farther north than California in the eastern north Pacific. For fifty years, the only false killer whale documented in the inland waters of Washington and British Columbia was one that was shot near Olympia in May of 1937. Then in early May of 1987, reports were received of an unidentified group of whales in southern Puget Sound. On May 5th, one of us, John Calambokidis, observed the animals and identified them as false killer whales. On that same day, a false killer whale also stranded in Carr Inlet in southern Puget Sound. This animal had been accompanied by a pod of approximately twelve others that were regularly observed feeding and playing in the waters between Vashon Island

57

A rare sight—two false killer whales feeding along the Tacoma shoreline. These whales were among a group of twelve that spent the spring of 1987 in lower Puget Sound.   FRED FELLEMAN

58

and Budd Inlet from the first week of May through June of 1987.

Canadian researchers also reported a false killer whale stranding that occurred during the first week of May of 1987. Initially thought to be a pilot whale, it was found stranded on the shores of Denman Island, British Columbia, in the northern reaches of Georgia Strait— over 150 miles north of Carr Inlet. These recent sightings in the inland waters have researchers wondering whether false killer whales are more prevalent in the inland waters than suspected. It could be that some of the unconfirmed reports of pilot whales from the last few decades were actually sightings of false killer whales, since the two species are extremely similar in appearance and tend to travel in similar-sized groups.

IDENTIFICATION False killer whales are normally found in the open ocean, traveling in schools of 100 or more. They are colored glossy black, except for a dark gray patch on the undersides that extends from the lower jaw to the area between the pectoral flippers and then tapers off near the belly. This gray patch is almost never visible at sea. These whales are about 6 feet in length at birth, with adult females reaching a maximum of 16 feet and males a maximum of about 20 feet. The head is rounded, with the upper jaw extending over the lower jaw by a few inches. The dorsal fin is curved, fairly large and located in the middle of the back; in adults, it reaches a height of approximately 15 inches. The pectoral flippers are unusual: near the point of attachment to the body, they bulge on the front edge and then taper off to a thin tip.

False killer whales can easily be confused with pilot whales and, to a lesser extent, with Risso's dolphins and possibly orcas. By way of contrast, orcas have larger dorsal fins and patches of bright white. Risso's dolphins

59

are colored gray to white in color, rather than the glossy black of the false killer whale, and pilot whales have a dorsal fin that is lower, wider at the base and situated somewhat closer to the blowhole than that of false killer whales. The pilot whale also has a gray saddle behind the fin and a more bulbous head that tends to plow through the water when it surfaces to breathe. Most distinctive are the false killer whale's overhanging upper jaw and oddly shaped pectoral fins, traits which it shares with no other species—but these features are almost never visible above the water's surface.

MICHAEL BIGG

BEAKED WHALES

MESOPLODON SPECIES

There are two species of *Mesoplodon* that could occur in the Greater Puget Sound region: *Mesoplodon stejnegeri*, the archbeak whale; and *M. carlhubbsi*, Hubb's beaked whale. Both of these species have been identified from strandings on the outer Washington coast. In the inland waters, only two strandings are known, both from the east side of Vancouver Island, and in neither case was it clear which species of *Mesoplodon* it was. The first

61

stranding is known only from a worn skull; the other—as seen at the beginning of this chapter—was a live animal that beached long enough to be photographed just outside the Pacific Biological Station at Nanaimo, British Columbia, before freeing itself and swimming away.

IDENTIFICATION The two *Mesoplodon* species are almost identical and thus are very hard to distinguish. Both have stocky bodies with small heads tapering to narrow beaks and small curved dorsal fins located along the back third of the body. Both are mostly black or grayish-brown in color and often have white oval scars and long scratches along the body. Adult male Hubb's beaked whales have a white forehead and a white beak, whereas some archbeak whales have light areas around the head. Adult male *Mesoplodons* have a single pair of large flattened teeth that protrude from the side of the lower jaw. These cetaceans occur singly or in groups of up to ten individuals. Newborns are probably about 6 feet in length and grow to 17 feet at maturity. Either species might be mistaken for a minke whale if only the back and dorsal fin are seen. The head of a minke is completely different, however, longer and broader and flat on top. *Mesoplodons* might also be confused with the goosebeak whale, but the goosebeak will have a shorter beak and, in males, conical teeth situated at the forward end of the lower jaw.

GOOSEBEAK WHALE (*Ziphius cavirostris*)

The goosebeak whale is common along the continental shelf from Baja California to the Aleutian Islands. Two strandings have been reported from the inland waters, both from the Strait of Juan de Fuca along Vancouver Island. Like all beaked whales, this species is only an accidental visitor to the inland waters.

IDENTIFICATION The goosebeak whale, also known as Cuvier's beaked whale, has a pointed rostrum with an indistinct beak. Its coloration is highly variable, centering around a rusty brown-to-tan color on top and dark to light brown on the undersides. Older animals are noticeably scarred and white around the head and back. In males only, there are two conical teeth at the tip of the lower jaw which are exposed when the mouth is closed. The dorsal fin is usually relatively tall (15 inches), curved and located well behind the mid-back. Calves are between 7 and 10 feet in length; adults reach 23 feet. Goosebeak whales usually travel in small groups of between two and six individuals. They may be confused with other beaked whales, especially with species of *Mesoplodon* and possibly with a young Baird's beaked whale, although it is unlikely that a young Baird's beaked whale would be traveling without adults. *Mesoplodon* whales have a longer beak and, in males, large flat triangular teeth located on the sides, not the tip, of the jaw. A young Baird's beaked whale can be distinguished from a goosebeak whale by its much more bulbous head and long beak. A goosebeak whale could also be confused with a minke whale, but the minke whale has a longer, broader, flattened head.

BAIRD'S BEAKED WHALE (*Berardius bairdii*)

Baird's beaked whale, also known as the North Pacific giant bottlenose whale, is relatively common outside the continental shelf along the Washington and British Columbia coasts. The only record of its occurrence in the inland waters is of a stranded female near Port Townsend, Washington, in December of 1962.

IDENTIFICATION Baird's beaked whales are normally found in groups of six to forty individuals. The body is long and cigar-shaped with a small triangular dorsal fin

63

located well behind the mid-back. The long beak of this marine mammal is accentuated by a steeply bulbous forehead, and the lower jaw extends beyond the upper jaw. These whales are bluish-gray, brown or black on top and gray to white on the undersides, with light-colored mottling on the sides. Newborns are approximately 15 feet in length; adults reach a maximum of 42 feet. Two triangular teeth protrude from the tip of the lower jaw in all but the youngest animals, and these teeth may be visible when identifying this species at sea. Because of its large size, bulbous head and long beak, the Baird's beaked whale is unlikely to be confused with any other species in this part of the world.

HOWARD WINN

PYGMY SPERM WHALE
Kogia breviceps

Pygmy sperm whales are slow-moving oceanic whales that are reportedly easy to approach by boat, if you are ever lucky enough to encounter them. They probably occur in local waters only when they are sick and searching for a place to strand. There have been three strandings recorded locally: one on the outer Washington coast in May of 1942; and two in the inland waters—the first on the east side of Whidbey Island near Oak Harbor in October of 1977, and the second at Port

65

Angeles in the eastern Strait of Juan de Fuca in June of 1985. In both of the recent strandings, the bodies were fairly fresh, so the animals had probably entered the inland waters while still alive and had not drifted in dead from the ocean. It is very unusual to see one of these animals; they are considered rare even within their normal range.

IDENTIFICATION The pygmy sperm whale is short and stout, dark brown to black on top, fading to gray on the sides and almost white on the belly. Newborns are about 4 feet in length; adults reach a maximum of 11 feet. Just behind the eyes is a crescent-shaped dark marking that resembles the gill slit of a fish. The blow-hole is at the left front of the squared-off head. This species is rarely seen, except in very calm water; its blow is not visible and normal surfacing is inconspicuous. Like all members of the sperm whale family, its narrow lower jaw is underslung. The lower jaw contains ten to sixteen curved needle-sharp teeth on either side which fit into sockets in the upper gum. There are no teeth in the upper jaw. The pectoral fins are relatively large, rounded at the tip with a small notch in the middle of the following edge. The small curved dorsal fin is located to the rear of the mid-back. The fin might lead an observer to mistake a pygmy sperm whale for a small minke or a small beaked whale. A good view of the squared shape of the pygmy sperm whale's head and consideration of its extremely small size should clarify the identity.

66

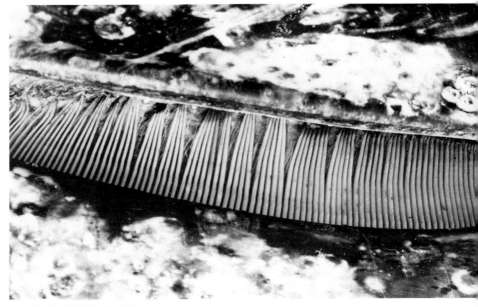

BALEEN WHALES

Suborder Mysticeti

Baleen whales include three families (eleven species) worldwide, ranging in size from the pygmy right whale at about twenty feet in length to the blue whale at more than 100 feet. They all have double blowholes and, instead of teeth, a unique apparatus for filtering food— plates of horny baleen that hang from the upper jaw, several hundred on each side of the mouth. The fringed edges of these baleen plates form a sieve that allows the mysticete to feed on very small prey, such as planktonic

67

crustaceans or baitfish. Stiff but flexible, baleen was one of the main incentives for commercial hunting of these whales in the days before plastics. It was used for corset stays, buggy whips and umbrella ribs, among other things. As a result of whaling, eight of the eleven baleen whale species have been so depleted that they are considered endangered, and most of these are now protected from commercial hunting.

Most baleen whales migrate regularly between colder waters in the summer where they feed and warmer waters in the winter where they mate and bear their young. Gestation is usually about one year and the calves, born singly, are nursed for six months to a year, depending on the species. In many cases, the female is fasting (not feeding) during the last months of pregnancy and the first months of lactation. This remarkable metabolic feat is made possible only by the energy stored in the whale's blubber while on the summer feeding grounds.

Six species from three families of the baleen whales have been reported in Greater Puget Sound and are described in the following pages. Two are common at present: the gray whale, lone representative of the family Eschrichtiidae; and the minke whale of the family Balaenopteridae (rorquals)—a group characterized by flat heads, small dorsal fins and long throat grooves that expand during feeding. A third species, the humpback whale, is also a Balaenopterid; it was once common in the inland waters but is rare today. Three more species have been reported but are extremely rare: the sei whale and the fin whale, also of the family Balaenopteridae; and the highly endangered northern right whale—a rotund member of the family Balaenidae, a group known for its long baleen, strongly arched jaw and lack of dorsal fin and throat grooves.

NATIONAL MARINE FISHERIES SERVICE

GRAY WHALE
Eschrichtius robustus

The gray whale is probably the best known cetacean on the west coast of North America because of its annual migrations north and south within viewing distance of land. It has recovered from heavy hunting more dramatically than any other baleen whale. Twice reduced to precariously low levels by commercial whalers, the gray whale in the eastern North Pacific may be as numerous today—at 15,000 to 20,000 whales—as it was before the start of commercial whaling. Gray whales regularly enter our inland waters in small numbers on their way up and down the outer coast. A few individuals may be year-round residents.

69

A barnacled back and knobbed dorsal ridge is as much as you will usually see of a gray whale in Greater Puget Sound. JOHN CALAMBOKIDIS

IDENTIFICATION The gray whale, which is about 16 feet long at birth and about 46 feet long at maximum size, has no dorsal fin. Instead it has a series of six to twelve low knuckle-like knobs that begin where a dorsal fin would be and extend backwards along the tailstock. In color, it is mottled gray, sometimes with patches that are very pale or even white. Infestations of barnacles and whale lice, especially on the head and back, contribute to its unkempt appearance, as do many small indentations on the head. The gray whale's head is quite narrow; the jawline is slightly arched; and the top of the head is somewhat rounded with no median ridge. The throat has just a few (two to five) short pleats.

The blow of a gray whale is fairly low and bushy but usually visible from considerable distances. The flukes, mottled like the rest of the body, are often raised before a long dive. When feeding, this cetacean may surface with mud on its head, amid clouds of billowing muddy water.

Due to its size and lack of a dorsal fin, the gray whale

is likely to be confused only with the right whale (especially a right whale with gray mottling from peeling skin) or the occasional humpback whale with a very reduced dorsal fin. In contrast, right whale heads carry callosities—raised patches of roughened skin—that are larger and rougher than the barnacles on a gray whale's head. Right whales also have strongly arched jawlines and lack the knobbed dorsal ridge of the gray whale. Humpback whales have very long pectoral fins, a flattened head with low smooth bumps and a serrated trailing edge to the tail flukes.

NATURAL HISTORY The annual migrations of gray whales are among the longest undertaken by any mammal—up to 7000 miles each way. Winters are spent in the protected lagoons of Baja California, where mating occurs and most of the calves are born. In spring, the whales head north up the coast to Alaska, through Unimak Pass in the Aleutian Islands and on to the Bering, Chukchi and Beaufort Seas for feeding. A small percentage of them stop for the summer to feed at places farther south along the migration route, such as Vancouver Island, the Strait of Juan de Fuca and as far south as northern California. In fall, the whales travel south again, close to shore most of the way, back to the warm Mexican waters.

Females probably bear calves once every two years and nurse them for seven to eight months. At birth, gray whales are about 16 feet in length. Mothers with newborn calves stick to the innermost shallow waters of the lagoons, avoiding the boisterous mating groups in deeper water, and the mother-calf pairs migrate north a month after most other whales. They are no longer paired up on the return migration south in the fall.

Gray whales, unlike other baleen whales, usually feed on the ocean bottom. They take a remarkable variety of

71

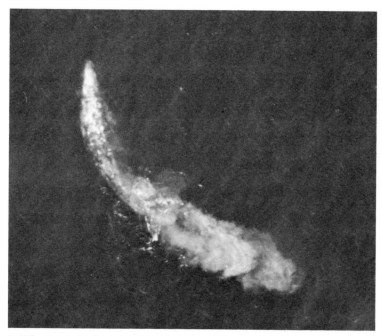

With a mud plume in its wake, a bottom-feeding gray whale is photographed from the air.   JOHN CALAMBOKIDIS

prey, in part because they often scoop up mouthfuls of bottom sediment and filter from it all the larger living organisms in the mud. When feeding in this manner, they leave large pits on the ocean floor, and they surface between mouthfuls amid great plumes of muddy water. Although amphipod crustaceans are the predominant prey in many areas, gray whales can also take dense concentrations of other animals, such as polychaete worms, crab larvae or small fish. Some of the prey are open-ocean rather than bottom dwellers, and it is also possible that at times gray whales even feed on seaweed and other plants. Perhaps this cetacean's ability to exploit a variety of prey has contributed to its recovery (in our area, at least) from the severe overhunting of the nineteenth century. However, a second population of gray whales on the western side of the North Pacific still remains at precariously low numbers from earlier hunting in this region.

Those who hunted gray whales in the nineteenth century found their quarry to be aggressive and dangerous when struck with the first harpoon, more so than other large whales. Boats were capsized and smashed, and men were killed. Those who survived called the gray whales "devil fish" and "hard heads." Within the past ten years, people have again started pursuing gray whales—this time just to watch, photograph and admire them. In the lagoons of Baja California and occasionally farther north, gray whales are responding to boats with a non-aggressive curiosity of their own—swimming very close, rubbing and nudging the boat. Often they let the passengers pat their mottled heads. Instead of devil fish, "friendly" is now the common description for gray whales.

Individual gray whales may be recognized by the

Gray Whale Distribution

complex pattern of mottling on the body, which is unique to each individual animal and stable over time. Research on the outer coast of Vancouver Island has shown that individuals tend to return to the same area to feed summer after summer. Only sporadic research has been conducted on gray whales in the inland waters of Washington State, so we do not know whether the same individuals return year after year, or whether we just see casual strays. A study by Cascadia Research along the United States side of the Strait of Juan de Fuca indicates that gray whales, mostly yearlings, will remain and feed in the area for up to four months. Most of the strandings that have occurred in the inland waters during the last ten years have been yearling males.

LOCAL DISTRIBUTION   Gray whales are currently seen with some regularity in Greater Puget Sound, with sightings recorded for every month and every year since 1976. Their peak abundance here extends between December and April, which suggests that most of them are using the inland waters as a temporary diversion during migration both north and south along the outer coast. However, gray whale sightings continue year-round in Greater Puget Sound, indicating that a few of them use the area as a summering ground. Additionally, during winter months between the main migration times of December and March, local sightings of gray whales may represent individuals that are either too young or too old to participate in the full migration to the breeding and calving grounds.

When gray whales are sighted in the inland waters, they are often reported for a few consecutive days or weeks in the same area. In Puget Sound, they are usually seen in shallow bays with muddy bottoms. In these areas, they are probably bottom-feeding on amphipods and other organisms dwelling in the sediment. In the

A gray whale lifts its barnacled flukes for a deep dive which will last about 5 minutes. The barnacles are a species unique to this marine mammal. JAMES DARLING/WEST COAST WHALE RESEARCH FOUNDATION

Strait of Juan de Fuca near Neah Bay, they are regularly seen year-round within three miles of shore, where they may be feeding on mysids, fish larvae, small schooling fishes and amphipods.

HOW TO OBSERVE Gray whales are best observed from shore as they migrate along the coast, especially in March and April as they travel north and come in quite close to shore. During migration south in November and December, the grays move farther off shore and are more difficult to see. Along Washington's outer coast, Moclips, Kalaloch and especially Cape Flattery are good gray whale-watching spots. On Vancouver Island, Long Beach between Ucluelet and Tofino is the best viewing area. During the migration seasons, gray whale-watching cruises are also available out of Westport in Washington and Tofino on Vancouver Island.

Within the inland waters, shore-based sightings of gray whales are far from predictable, but if you are at the

75

right place at the right time you can observe the whales for hours as they feed in the shallow bays of Puget Sound and along the shorelines of the Strait of Juan de Fuca. When observing gray whales from a vessel, the basic whale-watching guideline should be followed: do not approach closer than 100 yards. Some gray whales are known as "friendly whales" because they have learned to enjoy being rubbed and scratched by whale watchers in inflatable boats on the breeding grounds of Baja California. Some of these friendly whales make their way into our local waters and will swim right up to boats idling in the water. If you are approached by one of these friendly gray whales while watching from 100 yards away, it is not illegal to pet them if they actually come up to your boat. But leave your motor idling; they seem to like the sound of a boat engine, and it helps ensure that the whale knows where your boat is, so it will not accidently hit it. Then, when the whale has decided to leave, do not engage your motor until it has moved at least 100 yards away. Under the unlikely circumstance that a friendly gray whale will not leave your boat alone, slowly drive away and then increase speed after you have passed the 100-yard limit.

FRED FELLEMAN

MINKE WHALE
Balaenoptera acutorostrata

The minke whale (pronounced "minky") is the most common baleen whale in the inland waters, but it can be inconspicuous. A typical minke whale sighting consists of only two or three glimpses of something that looks like an overgrown dolphin. When minke whales are feeding, however, they can put on quite a spectacular show, executing vigorous lunges or half-breaches as they pursue baitfish.

IDENTIFICATION The minke whale is usually recognized as a solitary, medium-sized cetacean with a prominent, curved dorsal fin set far back on the body. It may reach 30 feet in length, but minke whales in the inland waters are usually shorter. Its blow is rarely visible, except under unusual lighting conditions or extreme cold, but it is audible for quite a distance on a calm day.

77

The minke's most distinctive field mark—which sets it apart from all other whales—is the white band on its pectoral fin. This band is visible through the water only at close range to an observer standing well above the water's surface, as on the bridge of a purse seiner.

When the minke surfaces for air, it often shows the shape of its head—sharply pointed at the tip and smooth and flat on top, except for a single median ridge leading forward from the blowholes. The dorsal fin is located far enough back on the body that the blowholes are just about to disappear under water as the dorsal fin emerges on a normal surfacing. The tail flukes are not raised above water on a dive.

With small fish streaming from its mouth, a minke whale lunges upside down at the surface. A. RUS HOELZEL

Minke whales are dark gray or brownish in color dorsally (not as black as orcas), with swaths of paler gray on the sides. The white belly and the throat pleats may be visible when the whale breaches or lunges after food. It is unlikely that anyone would confuse a minke whale with either of the two larger baleen whales that might be expected in Greater Puget Sound—the gray whale and the humpback whale—because both of these species produce visible blows that are large enough to be seen from over a mile away. Furthermore, neither of these local whales have the prominent curved dorsal fin of the minke. Killer whales and pilot whales are about the same size as minke whales and have similarly indistinct blows, but both of these species have shorter heads that are rounded rather than flat, and both have larger dorsal fins that are set farther forward on the body. Both also usually travel in groups, whereas minke whales are usually solitary. From a distance, it might be difficult to distinguish between a minke whale and a lone female or immature killer whale. Watch for the greater extent of back that is visible in front of the dorsal fin in the minke whale. Some species of beaked whales, which are extremely rare in these waters, could easily be confused with a minke, based on the location and relative size of the dorsal fin. However, the beaked whales have shorter and narrower heads, with rounded foreheads and distinct beaks, in contrast to the flat head of the minke.

NATURAL HISTORY Minke whales are the most numerous baleen whales on earth today, and they are widely distributed around the world. In the Antarctic, they feed mostly on krill, while in other areas they may consume small fish, copepods or squid. Each summer, minke whales migrate to feeding grounds in higher latitudes, but their winter distribution and behavior are poorly known. No one has ever reported seeing mating or calving for this species, but both are presumed to occur in winter at lower latitudes and in warmer water than on the feeding grounds.

Minkes are 8 to 9 feet long at birth and reach a

79

maximum length of about 30 feet in the Northern Hemisphere. At maturity, they may weigh up to 10 tons. They reach sexual maturity when they are 22 to 25 feet in length, but their age at this time is uncertain; estimates vary from three years to eight years of age. Females produce one calf every one to two years and nurse them for a shorter period than other baleen whales—only for four to six months.

Data from the commercial hunting of minke whales show that these cetaceans tend to segregate by age and sex more than other species of baleen whales. However, because it is not possible to tell a male from a female minke in the wild, we cannot say whether the minke whales in Greater Puget Sound are predominantly one sex or the other.

Except in the Antarctic, where schools of over 100 minke whales have been observed, these whales appear to be mostly solitary when on their feeding grounds. Pairs or even trios may occasionally swim side by side for brief periods, but, if two or more are in the same area, they usually appear to act independently of each other.

In the San Juan Islands, minke whales feed on small schooling fish—herring and probably sand lance. Two distinct methods of feeding have been observed. In one type, the minke whale hunts a school of fish at considerable depth and drives it to the water's surface. As the minke rises to gulp a mouthful of prey, its momentum thrusts it part way out of the water in a lunge or a half-breach that may reveal its greatly distended throat. In the second type of feeding, the minke takes small fish that have already been concentrated at the surface by feeding seabirds and perhaps larger fish. When this happens, the noisy flock of gulls and alcids will suddenly lift into the air just before the minke whale surfaces beneath them, taking their meal away. Individual minke whales tend to specialize in one or the other of these two feeding methods.

Minke whales are sometimes preyed upon by orcas. One description of such an attack in Barkley Sound on Vancouver Island suggests that the minke was killed by drowning—by being held underwater by the killer whales. In Greater Puget Sound, only transient killer whale pods would likely try to take a minke whale, since the resident pods here feed primarily on salmon and other fish. This may explain why minkes and killer whales appear to share the same waters peacefully most of the time. In the San Juan Islands, individuals of the two species have been seen passing within a body length of each other with no visible reaction, and in Johnstone Strait, British Columbia, a minke whale has been seen swimming with a small group of orcas.

In the 1980s, the minke became the most heavily hunted whale in the world, with catches off Japan, Korea, Norway, Iceland, Greenland, Brazil and Antarctica. An average of 10,000 minkes were taken every year during the first half of the decade. Large scale, factory-ship whaling of minkes in the Antarctic began only in 1971, after depletion of the larger species of baleen whales. Small scale, shore-based hunting of minkes, however, has a long history throughout the world.

Individual minke whales can be recognized by the shape of the dorsal fin, the distribution of small scars and the pattern of pale pigmentation on the sides. Research in the San Juan Islands has identified twenty-eight minke whales there since 1980. A catalog of these individuals begins on page 179 of this field guide.

LOCAL DISTRIBUTION Minke whales are seen in numerous locations in northern Puget Sound, the San Juan Islands and the Gulf Islands. Sightings in southern Puget Sound and the Strait of Juan de Fuca are more rare.

Pale swaths along the minke whale's sides are important individual markings used in photo-identification. This individual is known as Pancho Villa.　　　　　A. RUS HOELZEL

Studies in the San Juan Islands have identified four feeding areas where minkes may be found fairly regularly in summer and early fall. These are: Hein Bank, Salmon Bank, San Juan Channel (in the vicinity of Pear Point on San Juan Island) and south and west of Sandy Point on Waldron Island. There are probably other feeding areas in Greater Puget Sound, and there is some year-to-year variation in the use of some of these areas by the minke whales. During the past several summers, for example, the last two feeding areas mentioned above were not reliable places for finding minkes. This may reflect fluctuations in the local abundance of prey.

The minke whale population in these waters peaks between July and September, and there are very few seen in winter months. Their winter range is unknown, but individuals tend to return to the same places in the San Juan Islands summer after summer. Minke whale calves are almost never seen in these waters, except as occasional strandings in spring.

HOW TO OBSERVE When searching for a minke whale, it is best to use your ears as well as your eyes. Scan

82

the waters from a quiet boat (the calmer the water, the greater the chance of seeing a whale) and listen for a blow. If you find a minke that is traveling from one place to another, you may be able to follow it for several miles by maintaining its direction and speed while the whale is underwater. Keep at a respectful distance (100 yards) when the whale surfaces, so as not to disturb it. Minkes commonly travel quite slowly, at about one knot, surfacing several times in a row fifteen to forty-five seconds apart, then diving for up to eight to ten minutes (sometimes even longer) before the next surfacing series. The trick is not to give up during the long dives. The start of a long dive is often signaled when the minke whale makes a strong arch in its tailstock as it submerges, thus lifting the tailstock higher than usual out of the water.

When a minke is milling about and feeding, however, it is harder to follow, because it moves unpredictably within a couple of square miles. Its direction of movement underwater then bears no relation to its heading at the surface. The best strategy in this situation is to stay

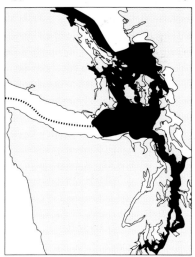

Minke Whale Distribution

83

near the location of the last surfacing and wait for the next one, so that you know which direction to take. If a minke whale is breach-feeding or lunge-feeding, there is the remote chance that it might lunge into your boat by mistake, so you may want to make some noise— idling the motor or tapping the hull—to tell it where you are. If there are seabirds feeding in the vicinity of a minke whale, keep an eye on the birds as the possible place for the whale's next surfacing, but do not get too close, because the surfacing could be vigorous.

Occasionally a minke whale will pass close to a boat to take a look, usually just once. This is more likely to happen if the boat is quiet in the water.

A minke whale strains water from a throat full of herring off San Juan Island.   A. RUS HOELZEL

FRED FELLEMAN

HUMPBACK WHALE
Megaptera novaeangliae

The humpback whale is the great singer among whales. Its long complex songs have inspired musicians, intrigued scientists and delighted the world. Once, this species was common in the inland waters of Washington and British Columbia, but local whalers wiped it out after the turn of the century. We can hope that the occasional sightings of the past ten years are harbingers of the humpback's return to our area.

IDENTIFICATION The humpback whale is a large cetacean—up to 52 feet in length—with a small dorsal fin that varies in shape from a triangular bump to a distinctly sickle-shaped curve. Sometimes the ridge of the tailstock behind the dorsal fin carries small knuckle-

85

like bumps. The pectoral fins are longer than those of any other cetacean—over one-fourth the length of the body. They are irregularly knobbed on the leading edge and very flexible. Like all rorquals, humpbacks have many long ventral grooves or throat pleats that allow the throat to expand when the whale is feeding.

Revealing the distinctive knobs on its head, a humpback comes up for air with its double blow holes open. BARBARA TODD

The humpback's head is flattened on top, with a median ridge; it is U-shaped at the tip when viewed from above. A number of low smooth knobs (called "stove bolts" by whalers) are scattered over the top of the head and the upper part of the lower jaw. The lower jaw also carries an irregular fleshy protuberance near the tip.

Humpbacks are black or dark slate-gray on top with a variable amount of white underneath, including the flippers. The undersides of the tail flukes may be all white, partially white or all black. The flukes are often raised on a deep dive, thus showing the undersides and the irregularly serrated trailing edge. It is not uncommon to see large white barnacles, or the scars from them, scattered on the head, as well as over other parts of the body, especially on the flippers and flukes.

Humpback whales produce a blow that is usually visible and quite bushy in appearance. At times, they are very active at the surface—breaching, flipper slapping and tail lobbing—thus enhancing their visibility, as well as their interest to the whale-watching public.

The humpback's small dorsal fin resembles that of only one other large whale that might occur locally— the fin whale. The fin whale can be distinguished by much shorter pectoral fins, a head with no knobs and a blow that is taller and thinner than that of the humpback. Also, fin whales do not lift their flukes to dive as humpback whales often do. The occasional humpback whale with a dorsal fin reduced to little more than a bump might also be confused with the gray whale, especially if its tailstock is knobbed. However, gray whales are colored a mottled gray all over, have much shorter pectoral fins and rather narrow heads that are somewhat rounded.

NATURAL HISTORY Humpback whales congregate both in summer and in winter at the ends of their annual migration routes, usually not far from shore. In the eastern North Pacific, they winter and bear their young in the Hawaiian Islands or along the west coast of Mexico. They spend their summers along the west coast of the United States and Canada.

Winter, the season for mating and calving, is also the time when humpbacks do most of their singing. If you swim underwater in humpback haunts around the Hawaiian Islands, you can hear their songs ring through the water, even when no whale is in sight. Phrases repeat, then change to the phrases of the next theme and then to the next, eventually returning to the start with no break. The song usually lasts from five to twenty minutes and may contain up to nine different themes. Humpback whales in the North Atlantic or in the South

Pacific sing a completely different song from those in the North Pacific, but, in Hawaii and off Mexico, the song is the same at any one time. Most astonishing is the fact that the themes change gradually over time, so that after five years the song is completely unrecognizable. No other animal song is known to evolve over time quite like the humpback's song.

Usually, and perhaps exclusively, the singers are lone males, and they appear to sing as part of mating behavior, perhaps to attract females. During this season, males in boisterous groups will, at times, fight over females, with powerful lashes of the tail that sometimes draw blood. Females can have calves as often as every year and the mother-calf pairs usually stay in shallow water close to shore. Humpback calves are about 15 feet in length at birth.

In contrast to the aggressive behavior seen in winter, summering humpbacks sometimes appear to cooperate in feeding on their usual diet of small schooling fish or krill. They use a variety of techniques to concentrate

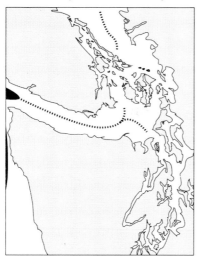

Humpback Whale Distribution

and capture their prey, including exhaling bubbles in lines or circles which act as a net. The food is taken in a huge mouthful, with the whale's throat greatly distended. Although individual humpback whales have been seen returning year after year to the same feeding grounds, a feeding area may be suddenly emptied of humpbacks if the prey drops dramatically.

LOCAL DISTRIBUTION The humpback whale is not now a regularly occurring species in the inland waters of Greater Puget Sound, but it has been in the past. In the early part of this century, there was a productive commercial hunt for humpbacks in Georgia Strait that was probably responsible for their disappearance from local waters. Since 1976, only three humpback sightings have been reported in the inland waters. In May of 1976, two individuals were sighted south of Whidbey Island in Puget Sound proper; in 1978, four individuals were sighted in this same region; and in June of 1986, what appeared to be a lone individual was tracked from south of Tacoma up into Saanich Inlet on southern Vancouver Island in a series of four sightings over six days.

On Juan de Fuca Bank and La Perouse Bank, 30 to 40 miles offshore of Washington and Vancouver Island, humpbacks have been regularly reported during July and August during the last decade. Feeding groups of up to five whales have been documented on the banks. However, field studies in this area have yet to be initiated, so whether these offshore humpback sightings represent a consistent summer population or only sporadic groups is still unknown. It is reasonable to expect that, like the recovering gray whales, the North Pacific population of humpbacks will increase under international protection and so will their occurrence in local coastal and inland waters.

HOW TO OBSERVE: Humpback whales have been

89

seen so rarely in our waters in recent years that it is unlikely that you will see one and impossible to suggest locations where they might be found. If you should come across a humpback whale, however, a couple of tips may help. Humpbacks often surface to breathe several times in rapid succession and then make a longer, deeper dive before the next surfacing. As the humpback starts the long dive, it will often raise its tail flukes out of the water, so be prepared to wait for awhile—perhaps ten minutes or even more. To find the whale when it resurfaces, scan the water for the highly visible blow and listen as well, because the blows are audible over long distances in calm conditions. As with other marine mammals, remember not to approach a humpback whale closer than 100 yards.

Like a human fingerprint, the markings on a humpback's flukes can be used to identify individuals. This one is Humphrey, a wayward whale who wandered up the Sacramento River in 1985.

JOHN CALAMBOKIDIS

JOHN CALAMBOKIDIS

SEI WHALE
Balaenoptera borealis

The sei (pronounced "say") whale was considered by whalers to be the fastest of the baleen whales. Mostly oceanic in its distribution, this species has been reported as a rare visitor to the inland waters but not since the 1940s. When the larger fin whale declined in the 1960s, due to local overexploitation, the sei whale became the most numerous baleen whale processed at the last whaling station on Vancouver Island. Currently sei whales are fairly abundant off the coast of Washington and British Columbia during summer months, but, due to their oceanic habits, they will probably always remain rare visitors to the inland waters.

IDENTIFICATION The sei whale can be difficult to identify at sea. It is a large whale, up to 60 feet in length, with a prominent, curved dorsal fin. Calves are about 15

91

feet long at birth. The sei whale looks like an overgrown minke whale, but, unlike the minke, its blow is consistently visible. The head is slightly rounded, both at the tip and at the sides, and there is a single median ridge in front of the blowholes. In color, sei whales are mostly dark gray, even on the undersides of the flukes, the flippers and the tailstock. A small amount of white on the ventral area is restricted to the throat and the forward portion of the belly, and there may be a swath of pale gray on the sides, similar to the minke whale. Many sei whales in the North Pacific are spotted with small pale oval scars which are probably caused by cookie-cutter sharks. Sei whales often swim near the surface just before and after surfacing, with the result that a trail of "fluke prints" can often be seen when the animal is underwater.

On the rare occasion when it strays into our inland waters, the sei whale might be mistaken for the equally rare fin whale or for a minke whale. Minke whales are noticeably smaller animals, however, and rarely produce a visible blow. Minkes also have a characteristic white band on the pectoral fin, a very pointed, flat head and a dorsal fin that is smaller and located somewhat farther back on the body. Fin whales may overlap in size with sei whales, but they have white pigmentation on the right side of the head where sei whales are dark. Fin whales also have a dorsal fin that is noticeably smaller than that of the sei whale, and it is set somewhat farther back on the body.

CENTER FOR COASTAL STUDIES

FIN WHALE
Balaenoptera physalus

The fin whale was the most abundant baleen whale taken commercially off British Columbia during most of this century. In the early 1960s, it almost completely disappeared from the area, probably due to overexploitation. Prior to this, fin whales were occasional summer visitors to the inland waters. At the northern end of Vancouver Island, a resident fin whale was known to locals for over a decade until it was shot to death by an unidentified boater in the early 1970s. Most fin whales sighted in the Greater Puget Sound region have probably been migrants between feeding grounds farther north and breeding grounds to the south. The only fin whale documented for the inland waters in recent times was a dead individual that was pushed into Tacoma on the bow of a freighter in 1985.

IDENTIFICATION From a distance the fin whale looks like a very large whale with a small dorsal fin and a tall thin blow. It may grow to 80 feet in length (calves are 20 feet long at birth), and its dorsal fin is usually somewhat curved. The head is flattened on top with a single central ridge, and the tip of the head is less pointed than that of the minke whale.

Fin whales are colored mostly dark gray above and white below. The white coloration is asymmetrically distributed in a way not seen in any other whale: more white shows on the right side of the head than on the left side because the right lower lip is white (sometimes the right upper lip, as well). Also on the right side, a light wash extends from the lips to behind the blowholes. This pigmentation is illustrated in the photograph on the previous page. In contrast, the left side of the head is completely dark.

Behind the wash and the blowholes on the fin whale's back and "shoulder," there is more pale pigmentation—a chevron of pale gray that forms a "V" when viewed from above. The undersides of the flukes are white, but, because fin whales do not lift their flukes on a dive, the white undersides are visible only when the whale feeds on its side at the surface.

The fin whale can be confused with the humpback whale or the sei whale. Both of these cetaceans, however, have heads that are equally dark on both sides. The humpback also has smooth low bumps on its head and very long flippers, and it often lifts its flukes to dive. Distinguishing between a fin whale and a sei whale can be particularly difficult unless the head coloring is seen. The sei whale's blow is lower and its dorsal fin is more prominent than that of the fin whale. Also, the sei whale does not arch its back strongly in order to dive, whereas the fin whale often does.

ROGER PAYNE

NORTHERN RIGHT WHALE

Eubalaena glacialis

The right whale was so-named by early whalers because it was the "right" whale to catch: it had long baleen, thick blubber yielding much whale oil, and it floated when dead. Since right whales are fairly slow swimmers and congregate close to shore, they were also easy prey and were severely overhunted in all oceans. They have shown little sign of recovery, in spite of protection since 1937. Hence, this cetacean is considered the most endangered baleen whale. The entire population in the North Pacific is estimated at fewer than 300 animals.

Right whales have been identified in local archaeological remains, but they have never been considered common in the Greater Puget Sound region. The only recent sighting close to this area was on Swiftsure Bank at the entrance to the Strait of Juan de Fuca, where two

95

right whales were spotted in 1983. Of course, any further sightings would be of great interest.

IDENTIFICATION The right whale has several distinctive field marks. It has no dorsal fin. As illustrated in the photograph of a southern right whale on the previous page, its head bears unique roughened patches of skin called callosities, the largest of which is at the tip of the rostrum; and its jawline is strongly arched to accommodate very long baleen. Right whales may reach 55 feet in length, and newborn calves are about 15 feet long. Adults produce a large blow that is distinctly V-shaped. The skin is black, sometimes somewhat mottled by gray peeling. On the belly of most right whales is a white patch that is highly variable in size and shape. Some whales also have a white blaze on the back. The callosities on the head are paler than the black skin; they can be white or gray or somewhat yellow or orange, depending on the density of the whale lice that populate these protuberances. The pectoral fins are quite broad, and the tail flukes are often lifted in a dive.

No other large whale in these waters presents a smooth back without a dorsal fin or dorsal ridge. The bowhead whale, a close relative, also lacks a dorsal fin, but its range does not extend this far south. The gray whale is probably the only local species that might be confused with a right whale, but its knobby dorsal ridge and strongly mottled pale gray coloring should make the distinction clear.

Orca Rising MARK LEWIS

Cavorting Orcas   SUSAN KLEINBERG

Bow-riding Dall's Porpoises MICHAEL W. NEWCOMER

Minke Whale GILLIAN LANKSHEAR/OKEANOS

Gray Whales JAMES DARLING

Pilot Whale SUSAN H. SHANE

White-sided Dolphins   NATIONAL MARINE FISHERIES SERVICE

Harbor Seals STEVEN J. JEFFRIES

Rafting California Sea Lions PATRICK J. GEARIN

California Sea Lions GREGORY SILBER

Northern and California Sea Lions PATRICK J. GEARIN

Elephant Seal
THOMAS JEFFERSON

River Otter
TIMOTHY RANSOM

Pinnipeds

Pinnipeds—the seals, sea lions and walruses—are marine carnivores dependent on land for some portion of their lives. This contrasts with cetaceans—whales, dolphins and porpoises—which are totally independent of

97

land. For many pinniped species mating occurs on land, and almost all females leave the water to give birth and nurse their young. The term pinniped is derived from the Latin words *pinna*, for feathered or winged, and *ped*, for foot. This describes the adaptation of the limbs of these animals into paddles for swimming. Worldwide there are approximately thirty-four species of pinnipeds divided into three primary groups: the true or earless seals of the family Phocidae; the fur seals and sea lions of the family Otariidae; and the walrus of the family Odobenidae. Only five species from the first two groups occur in Greater Puget Sound: the harbor seal and the elephant seal (Phocidae); the California sea lion, the northern or Steller's sea lion and the northern fur seal (Otariidae).

TERRELL C. NEWBY

HARBOR SEAL
Phoca vitulina

While boating in Puget Sound, you may sometimes have the unsettling feeling that you are not alone. Don't be surprised to find the low profile of a harbor seal, eyes just above the water, staring at you from nearby. Just when you notice its presence, it is gone with scarcely a ripple, leaving you wondering what you saw.

Harbor seals are the most abundant and most commonly encountered marine mammals in the inland waters. They can be seen singly or in small groups in the

99

water where they will sometimes approach vessels, or they may be hauled out at any of dozens of sites regularly used for resting on land and giving birth to their young.

IDENTIFICATION The harbor seal is the smallest seal in Greater Puget Sound and the only one that is spotted. Its general coloration is highly variable, ranging from almost all tan or silver to black with white rings, but there are usually light or dark spots on some part of the body. It has a stubby compact body, with short front

Harbor seals often haul out on submerged rocks to rest, and sometimes they resemble logs from a distance. JON STERN

and rear flippers. A quick glance also reveals that it has no external ears—only small openings that are visible at close range. On land, it can also be identified by its awkward worm-like locomotion.

Harbor seals generally grow to 6 feet in length and a weight of about 200 pounds. Adult males tend to be slightly larger than females, although this difference is not apparent when observing them from a distance. The sexes can be distinguished only by close examination of their undersides—a procedure that is usually possible only when a dead animal is found on the beach. Along the undersides, about half-way between the front and rear flippers, is a small depression for the navel. Females will have two small protruding nipples about one-quarter of the way from the navel to the rear flippers. Males will have a penile opening half way between the navel and the rear flippers. Both the front and rear flippers are small and protrude only slightly from the rotund body. The short front flippers can barely reach the ground, and the rear flippers are fused so that they cannot be rotated under the body, as in sea lions. This reduces the harbor seal to a bouncing or wriggling motion when it moves on land.

The harbor seal can easily be distinguished from the three other pinnipeds that are common in the inland waters. Remember that it is earless, relatively small in size and spotted in color, unlike both of the larger sea lion species which have small furled ears and are solid in color. Its other earless relative, the northern elephant seal, is much larger, has an elongated snout and is mottled, rather than spotted. The harbor seal is also often seen in groups, while the northern elephant seal is only encountered singly in Greater Puget Sound.

NATURAL HISTORY Harbor seals occur all along the west coast of North America from Baja California to the Bering Sea, wherever sandspits, mudflats, icebergs, reefs and low rocks provide privacy and immediate access to the water. Their total population is about 300,000, with the majority occurring in Alaska.

Like all pinnipeds, harbor seals crawl out of the water to rest and give birth to their young. This process, called hauling out, occurs at specific sites that are used on a daily basis. Peak haul out usually occurs at low tide, although a high tide haul out is more common in Hood Canal.

101

A harbor seal pup feeds on its mother's fat-rich milk for its first four to six weeks of life.   STEVEN J. JEFFRIES

Female harbor seals become mature at three to five years of age, after which they give birth to a single pup every year. Mating occurs about one month after the birth of the previous pup, and there is a two-month delay between mating and the implantation of the embryo. The gestation from implantation to birth lasts nine months. Female harbor seals nurse their young on fat-rich milk for three to six weeks, during which time the pups more than double in weight—from just under 25 pounds to more than 50 pounds. This annual breeding cycle is usually similar in timing for all the seals breeding at any given location. Surprisingly, however, there are dramatic differences in breeding times within Washington State: pupping occurs in May and June on the outer Washington coast; in June and July in the Strait of Juan de Fuca and the San Juan Islands; and from July through September in southern Puget Sound and Hood Canal.

102

Although harbor seals consume fish, they are not restricted to any particular species, taking what is most abundant and easiest to catch in any particular area. In Greater Puget Sound, their diet includes more than twenty species of fish, with hake, pollock, sculpin, herring and tomcod being some of the most popular. One issue of major concern and controversy has been the harbor seal's predation on salmon. Until the early 1960s, the Washington State Department of Fisheries paid a bounty on harbor seals killed (about 17,000), primarily because of their purported predation on salmon. Continued research has revealed that harbor seal predation on free-swimming salmon is generally minimal and of little consequence in comparison to the human catch. On the other hand, harbor seal predation on already-caught salmon—in a gill net for example—can sometimes be high enough to have a major financial impact on individual fishermen.

Harbor seals generally do not live past thirty years, although "Dub Dub," a captive seal at Point Defiance Zoo and Aquarium, lived to thirty-three years. Adult males have a higher mortality than females, possibly because of stress and fighting during the annual mating season. The highest mortality occurs during the first few months after birth, with starvation, stillbirth and premature birth being the principal causes.

Pollutants—high concentrations of PCBs and DDT—may have also had an adverse impact on harbor seals. Although both of these chemicals have been banned in the United States and Canada, high concentrations still remain in some areas, including Greater Puget Sound. Marine mammals, including the harbor seal, are particularly vulnerable because they feed high on the food chain, consuming fish that are already loaded with these long-lasting contaminants. PCBs have been of particular concern because Puget Sound harbor seals have been found to carry some of the highest concentrations in the world—levels that could cause reproductive problems. In fact, during the 1970s, there was some evidence that the harbor seals in lower Puget Sound were having trouble reproducing—many pups were born prematurely or with birth defects—although a direct link to pollutants could not be proven. More recently, however, PCB levels in these animals appear to be dropping, at least in the younger seals, and harbor seals in the inland waters are increasing with no current reproductive problems. Although the rate of increase varies by region, it seems to average about ten percent per year. As a result, the harbor seal population has more than doubled in most areas during the last ten years. While this is good news for the seals and their supporters, fishermen who view harbor seals as competitors are finding the situation far from satisfactory.

LOCAL DISTRIBUTION Harbor seals are common in almost all waters of Greater Puget Sound, with a total

Harbor Seal Distribution

104

population for the region in excess of 5,000 animals year-round. Some of the highest concentrations occur in the San Juan Islands, where more than 2,000 harbor seals haul out on numerous scattered intertidal rocks and ledges. Another 1,000 harbor seals inhabit Hood Canal, primarily near major river deltas. In Puget Sound most harbor seals occur south of the Tacoma Narrows, with just under 1,000 seals in this area. Although harbor seals are known to move between sites at different seasons on Washington's outer coast, large scale seasonal movements do not appear to be as common in Greater Puget Sound.

HOW TO OBSERVE When harbor seals are hauled out, they are extremely wary of humans. Even your most cautious approach will be frustrating because the seals will enter the water when you are still about 100 yards away. Human encroachment can be very detrimental to these sensitive animals, particularly during the pupping season when disturbance may separate the mother from her newborn pup. In general, it is less intrusive to ob-

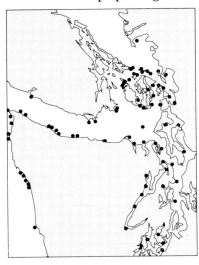

Harbor Seal Haul Out Sites

105

serve seals when they are in the water. At these times, they are less wary, and they may even approach your boat out of curiosity. They will approach closest if you are stationary and quiet. If you come upon seals hauled out, it is best to observe them from at least 100 yards' distance, using binoculars or a spotting scope. If they start to enter the water, this is a sign that you have approached too closely and should slowly retreat.

If you do not have a boat, there are several locations for harbor seal watching. A ferry ride through the San Juans within a few hours of low tide may provide a sighting or two. Train your binoculars on the barely exposed intertidal rocks and ledges off small islands on the north sides of Lopez and Shaw Islands. From shore, seal watching is best accomplished with a spotting scope. Along Hood Canal, try Highway 101 near high tide at the Duckabush or Hamma Hamma River deltas. In northern Puget Sound, scan the exposed mudflats at low tide in Samish and Padilla Bays for seals grouped along water channels in the mudflats.

STEVE FROHOCK

NORTHERN ELEPHANT SEAL
Mirounga angustirostris

The northern elephant seal is the largest and one of the most unusual pinnipeds that you will find in Greater Puget Sound. The unlikely beast in the photograph is one such example— an adult male swallowing a dog-fish. Slow-moving and lethargic, it resembles a dead-head at the surface when seen in the water. Though uncommon in Greater Puget Sound, a small number of these seals are regular seasonal visitors to the area.

107

IDENTIFICATION The northern elephant seal, which has an even larger counterpart in the Southern Hemisphere, is a giant among pinnipeds. Males are up to 20 feet in length and weigh as much as 8,000 pounds; females are much smaller in size, at 11 feet in length and up to 2,000 pounds. The skin is gray or brownish with little hair and no spots; it often appears in poor condition with portions sloughing off. Adult males, the usual visitors to Greater Puget Sound, have large protruding elephantine snouts and are often heavily scarred on the chest and neck. Like other true seals, the elephant seal has no ears and small front and rear flippers.

The elephant seal cannot easily be mistaken for any other pinniped. In contrast to the sea lions and fur seals, it has no external ears, and it cannot "walk" on its smaller flippers. It is much larger than its close relative, the harbor seal, and it lacks the spotted coat of this species. Although the protruding snout of the adult male is most distinguishable, even the smaller females and subadults have longer snouts than the harbor seal. In addition, elephant seals encountered afloat or hauled out in Greater Puget Sound are usually alone, and they may appear lethargic and non-responsive when approached. This behavior differs greatly from the more group-oriented and skittish habits of the harbor seal.

NATURAL HISTORY The elephant seal is generally a solitary oceanic species, although it comes ashore to breed and molt. In the Northern Hemisphere, this occurs on island and mainland beaches from central California to Mexico. The adult males usually come ashore first in December and the adult females arrive in late December and January. The females then give birth to a single pup and nurse it for slightly less than a month. During this period, the pup almost triples in weight, while the female fasts and survives off her fat

108

Elephant seals sometimes come ashore during their annual molt.
Pictured here is a yearling male.   JOHN CALAMBOKIDIS

reserves. In these sea mammals, mating occurs shortly after the pups are weaned. After the breeding season, some elephant seals migrate north as far as Alaska in search of feeding grounds.

Elephant seals are highly polygamous, and only a few dominant males breed with the majority of the adult females. This polygamous structure is more typical of the eared seals—the sea lions and fur seals—than the true seals, although dominant male elephant seals, unlike the eared seals, do not defend specific territories but groups of females instead. Elephant seals also come ashore for several weeks in the summer months for the annual molt. They slough off hair and skin in patches, and this gives them a blotchy appearance for a time.

109

Elephant seals are very deep divers, pursuing prey such as rays, squid, dogfish and other fish that favor deeper waters. Recent research on adult female elephant seals has revealed long dives lasting up to forty-seven minutes and extending to depths of over 2,500 feet.

The northern elephant seal was hunted to near extinction in the 19th century by commercial sealers. Only about 100 animals, isolated on one of the more remote breeding islands, survived the slaughter. Since that time, the northern elephant seal has made a remarkable comeback to an estimated current population of 100,000.

LOCAL DISTRIBUTION Northern elephant seals are relatively infrequent visitors to Greater Puget Sound, although several sightings are reported each year. Local sightings generally consist of solitary animals afloat or on a beach. Usually it is only the males and young of the year that venture north into the inland waters. They appear to be more common in the Strait of Juan de Fuca and the San Juan Islands than in other parts of the region, and, although most common in summer, they may occur here during any month of the year.

HOW TO OBSERVE The infrequent occurrence of elephant seals in the inland waters makes viewing them unlikely. In the water, they may be mistaken for deadheads or small buoys. When encountering them in the water, keep at least 100 yards' distance. If you come upon one lying motionless on land, be careful when approaching it. What may appear to be a dead or sick elephant seal may in fact be a healthy animal that is merely lethargic. If harassed, an elephant seal can move quickly to deliver a serious bite or injury.

110

PATRICK J. GEARIN

CALIFORNIA SEA LION

Zalophus californianus

There is nothing quiet or subtle about the California sea lion. This gregarious pinniped is usually loud, clever and unafraid—habits that have made it a popular performer in oceanariums and probably the best known of the pinnipeds. In perfect character, California sea lions have made a big splash in recent years as they have increased in Greater Puget Sound. These high-profile performers have succeeded in frustrating a variety of

111

California sea lions hitch a ride out of Seattle aboard a scow.

PATRICK J. GEARIN

state and federal agencies and received nationwide attention. "Oscar," a sea lion that was a regular visitor to Olympia, Washington, has often been photographed lounging on public docks or sunning himself in front of state office buildings. Another group of sea lions, under the collective name "Herschel," has undertaken forays after steelhead trout at Seattle's Hiram M. Chittenden Locks and succeeded in frustrating federal and state agencies trying to control them. Even the United States Navy has been humbled by sea lions that have crawled all over buoys at a local submarine acoustics base, disrupting sensitive tests with their loud barking.

IDENTIFICATION The California sea lion is dark brown or black in color and has the long front and rear flippers characteristic of sea lions and fur seals. Other identifying features are its small cone-shaped ears and lack of hair on the long flippers. California sea lions vary in size by sex. Adult males—the usual migrants into the inland waters—are up to 8 feet long and weigh up to 600 pounds. The males have a pronounced bump or crest on top of the head that is often a lighter color. The females, which are rarely seen in the inland waters, may be 6 feet in length and weigh up to 200 pounds. Both males and females produce a characteristic bark.

The California sea lion can easily be distinguished from other pinnipeds found in Greater Puget Sound. Its conical ears and large flippers indicate that it is not a true seal like the harbor seal or elephant seal. The two other members of its own family found locally—the northern sea lion and the northern fur seal— may be more difficult to differentiate. The northern sea lion, which is larger and usually much lighter in color, does not bark and has a broader head, without the crest of the adult male California sea lion. Its other relative, the northern fur seal, is rare in the inland waters; this pinniped does not bark, is much smaller, has a more pointed nose and more pronounced ears than the California sea lion.

NATURAL HISTORY Naturally agile and acrobatic, California sea lions swim with powerful motions of their front flippers and, when swimming rapidly, can "porpoise" through the water with ease at speeds up to 15 or 20 miles per hour. They are also expert divers, known to descend to depths of at least 450 feet. On land, these pinnipeds move easily and with surprising speed. They walk by alternating their long flippers, and they run in a sort of swaying motion by alternatively throwing the foreflippers forward and then bringing up both hind flippers.

The California sea lion breeds on island and mainland shores from central California to the tip of Baja California, including the Sea of Cortez. Pupping and breeding occur in May and June. The breeding system

113

is polygamous, with dominant adult males holding territories and mating with many females. These territories are established at locations on shore and in shallow water where females congregate or pass through while giving birth and nursing their pups. The females give birth to a single pup each year and nurse it intermittently between feeding trips out to sea. Although lactation normally lasts several months, sometimes yearling sea lions are still seen nursing from their mothers during the next breeding season. In fall, the males migrate as far north as British Columbia, while the females appear to stay in the vicinity of the breeding grounds. This movement each fall has shifted progressively farther north as the California sea lion population has increased in recent years. The growing population is currently at about 100,000, as legal protection permits this pinniped to recover from earlier exploitation.

There has been a great deal of publicity about sea lion predation on steelhead trout at the locks in Seattle. At this site, a relatively small number of sea lions has exacted a heavy toll on a small run of steelhead trout that must pass through the confined boat locks. This situation does not typify the California sea lion's diet: hake and herring are more common prey for this pinniped in Greater Puget Sound.

LOCAL DISTRIBUTION The historical population density of the California sea lion is difficult to determine because most early accounts did not differentiate between this species and the northern sea lion—although bones recovered from native villages indicate that it did occur in this region in the past. In this century, California sea lions were not documented in Washington until the 1950s, although a few must have passed through state waters because there were earlier sightings in British Columbia. From the 1950s through

1979, small but increasing numbers of California sea lions were known to congregate in Greater Puget Sound, particularly around Race Rocks in the Strait of Juan de Fuca. Since 1979, however, California sea lions in the inland waters have increased dramatically, with concentrations at Race Rocks, Porlier Pass in the Gulf Islands, Port Gardner near Everett, Elliott Bay in Seattle and near Fox Island in southern Puget Sound. During winter months at Port Gardner, as many as 1,000 California sea lions have been seen in recent years.

HOW TO OBSERVE California sea lions are relatively tolerant of humans, in contrast to more retiring pinnipeds like the harbor seal.You may suddenly see an inquiring head pop up near your boat or hear distant barks of animals hauled out on land. Despite their relative tolerance, sea lions should not be approached any closer than 100 yards. At this distance from a haul out site, it is unlikely that they will be startled into the water, as will harbor seals.

In addition to the major concentration areas already

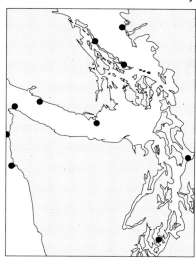

California Sea Lion
Main Haul Out
and Rafting Sites

115

A male California sea lion consumes a fish discarded by a fish buyer in Neah Bay.   JOHN CALAMBOKIDIS

mentioned above, California sea lions may be seen from land as they migrate in spring and fall along the south shore of the Strait of Juan de Fuca. During April and May, in particular, small groups can be seen traveling westward from almost any viewpoint along the north shore of the Olympic Peninsula. When the steelhead are running, the Hiram M. Chittenden Locks in Seattle is also a good site for observing California sea lions.

116

JAMES CUBBAGE

NORTHERN SEA LION
Eumetopias jubatus

The northern sea lion, also known as the Steller sea lion, is a larger, quieter relative of the California sea lion. Its broad head, deep throaty roar and golden color make it truly resemble a lion.

IDENTIFICATION Northern sea lions vary in size by sex, with males up to 10 feet long and weighing 2,200 pounds and females much smaller, at 7 feet and 600 pounds. The coat varies also—from a very light golden or yellow color to a brown that is almost as dark as the California sea lion. Older animals tend to be darker, and 117 adult males have broad, dark-colored and scarred chests. The posture and movements of northern sea lions are similar to those of the California sea lion.

Male sea lions in mixed company show their differences. The northern sea lion is larger and lighter in color. Its smaller relative, the California sea lion, is darker and has a pronounced crest on the forehead.   KARL KENYON

The northern sea lion is most easily confused with its cousin, the California sea lion. By way of contrast, the California sea lion is smaller and darker in color, and its head is much narrower, with a forehead crest in adult males. Vocalizations of these pinnipeds are also different: the northern sea lion is relatively silent except for an occasional low roar, while the California sea lion has a noisy and persistent bark. Northern sea lions can be distinguished from true or earless seals by their external ears, longer flippers, lighter color and their ability to stand and walk on their front and rear flippers.

NATURAL HISTORY   Northern sea lions are most numerous north of Washington as far as Alaska. Their breeding range extends from southern California to the Bering Sea. Strangely, there are no breeding colonies in Washington State, although they exist on the outer coasts of neighboring Oregon and British Columbia.

Like most other species of sea lions and fur seals, the northern sea lion is polygamous. Adult males control their territories at breeding rookeries where adult females congregate to give birth and nurse their young. The males have to defend these territories actively against other males through ritualized displays and, if the displays are not successful, occasional bloody fights. During the breeding season from mid-June to mid-August, adult males may stay on land defending their territories and not feed for sixty days. The females give birth to a single pup each year and, after nursing it intensely for about two weeks, alternate nursing the pup with feeding trips to sea.

The diet of northern sea lions includes various flat-fishs, cod, squid, octopus and rockfish. Salmon are taken occasionally, but they are not a major items of prey. However, sea lions feeding on netted salmon can be a problem for fishermen because their large size can result in major damage to the nets in which they become entangled. Northern sea lions also occasionally prey on other pinnipeds, including northern fur seal pups.

The northern sea lion population is now estimated at just under 200,000, with the great majority occurring in Alaska. In many areas, their populations have been declining drastically in recent years. Although the causes of this decline have not been determined, many sea lions are shot by fishermen or entangled in fishing nets and other gear.

LOCAL DISTRIBUTION Northern sea lions used to be far more numerous on the Washington outer coast than they are at present. Reports during the early 1900s indicated groups of several thousand at various rocks used as haul outs on Washington's outer coast. Currently northern sea lions congregate at Tatoosh Island on the outer coast, Sombrio Point and Race Rocks in the Strait of Juan de Fuca, Plumper Sound in the Gulf Islands, Sucia Island in the San Juan Islands and in southern Puget Sound. None of these areas are rookeries, nor are they much used by northern sea lions during the summer breeding season.

HOW TO OBSERVE Northern sea lions are generally more wary of humans than California sea lions. Those that are hauled out should not be approached closer than 100 yards; otherwise they may flee into the water. When they are in the water, they are not so timid and will sometimes approach vessels or lift themselves high out of the water for a better view. Northern sea lions can be seen at some of the locations mentioned above or

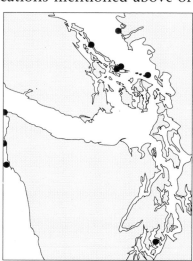

Northern Sea Lion
Main Haul Out Sites

120

A young northern sea lion poses regally, displaying its large flippers.
MARK LEWIS

121

from shore along the north side of the Olympic Peninsula in April and May when they migrate west out of the Strait of Juan de Fuca. Occasionally, during the winter and spring, they will rest temporarily on beaches, rocks or docks near remote shoreline residences. They should not be approached by foot, as they can be dangerously aggressive and can move very rapidly when startled on land.

KARL KENYON

NORTHERN FUR SEAL
Callorhinus ursinus

As one of the most oceanic pinnipeds, the northern fur seal spends about eight months of the year at sea without touching land. It is able to sleep at the surface, as in the photograph above, and would probably do well never coming ashore were it not for the requirements of breeding. Fur seals are extremely graceful and acrobatic in the water, able to clear the surface with a strong thrust of their front flippers.

Northern fur seals are the long-distance migrants of the pinniped world, traveling annually between their principal breeding grounds in the Bering Sea and feeding areas offshore of California, Oregon, Washington and British Columbia. The majority of northern fur seals breed in the summer on the Pribilof Islands, located in Alaska's Bering Sea.

123

"Monroe" discusses territory with a curious canine.

The northern fur seal has been one of the most heavily exploited pinnipeds. During the last century, its population has increased and decreased in response to various attempts at management and control. It is, at once, an example of our best successes and worst failures in the commercial exploitation of a species. During the last thirty years, northern fur seal populations have undergone a dramatic decline. Most evidence indicates that the cause is entanglement in the large number of non-degradable discarded pieces of fishing nets floating in the ocean.

Northern fur seals were extensively hunted by the Makah Indians from canoes at the entrance of the Strait of Juan de Fuca. Today stranded animals occasionally wash up on the outer coast, and every few years one is found in the inland waters. The most recent and most unusual stranding occurred some thirty miles from Puget Sound in 1987 at Monroe, Washington. In a cow

124

FRANK VARGA

pasture near Woods Creek, a young male fur seal was found, presumably having made his way up the Snohomish River to the Skykomish River and then to the creek. "Monroe," as he was named was released into the Sound a few days later. Although rarely encountered in the inland waters of Greater Puget Sound, northern fur seals feed and migrate in large numbers just off the coasts of Washington and British Columbia.

IDENTIFICATION Northern fur seals are generally gray to black in color. Females and juveniles are up to 5 feet in length and weigh as much as 135 pounds. Males are much larger (up to 600 pounds) but do not generally occur in the area, even off the coast of Washington or British Columbia. Like the other members of the eared seal family, the northern fur seal has small external ears and long front and rear flippers.

The northern fur seal may be confused with both the northern sea lion and the California sea lion. However,

125

northern sea lions are much larger and have a lighter coat; California sea lions are larger, the males have a conspicuous forehead crest and both sexes tend to be loud and vocal with their characteristic bark. As shown in the photo at the beginning of this chapter, the northern fur seal is often encountered resting in the water with the hindflippers and one or both foreflippers held in the air—a posture that old-time sealers called the "jug handle" position.

Mustelids

Mustelids—the weasels, minks, otters, ferrets and others of the family Mustelidae—are terrestrial carnivores usually associated with freshwater systems. The river and sea otters, however, both occur in the marine waters of Washington State and southern British Columbia and are therefore included here. Of these two, only the

127

sea otter is protected under the United States Marine Mammal Protection Act, while the river otter is still trapped in many areas.

The river otter, despite its name, is not restricted to river systems. It is far more common along the outer coasts and in the marine waters of Greater Puget Sound than the sea otter with which it is often confused. Sea otters rarely occur in Greater Puget Sound but are common along the outer coasts and occasionally may wander into the area. Minks, too, are sometimes seen feeding along the shorelines of the outer coast and inland waters and may be confused with river otters. However, unlike the otters, minks always appear to divide their livelihood between non-marine and marine habitats. Sea otters and some river otters, on the other hand, have become completely marine in their existence.

TIMOTHY RANSOM

RIVER OTTER
Lutra canadensis

A chance encounter with a river otter in the wild is one of the great treats of the natural world.   Active, intelligent and playful, this busy member of the weasel family is always entertaining to watch. Adapted to rivers, lakes, estuaries and even marine waters, it is common throughout most of Greater Puget Sound.   Despite its occurrence in marine waters, the river otter is not technically considered a marine mammal; hence, it is not afforded the legal protection of the United States Marine Mammal Protection Act. As a result, river otters

129

continue to be commercially trapped for their fur in Washington and British Columbia.

IDENTIFICATION The mature river otter weighs between 30 and 35 pounds and measures 4 to 4 1/2 feet in length. Its overall configuration can only be described as "weasel-shaped," coated with thick brown fur and topped by a small head and the muzzle of a mustelid. Its front and rear legs extend well out from the body, unlike the seals, and its toes are webbed. Its tail is long and slender, accounting for one-third of the body's length.

It is unlikely that the river otter would be confused with any other marine mammal, except the sea otter, or possibly, from a distance, a surfacing harbor seal. Many people assume that any otter seen in marine waters must be a sea otter, rather than a river otter. This is untrue, and if you should come upon either species, you will find that they are not very difficult to distinguish. The river otter is much smaller; unlike the sea otter, it has a brown rather than grayish face and a slender rather than stocky tail. It is never seen on its back in the water feeding, swimming or resting, as is the sea otter. Instead it hunts along both fresh and saltwater shores and even plays on docks and around boats in Greater Puget Sound. Since the sea otter is only a very rare visitor to the inland waters, most otters seen are river otters. In fresh water, river otters may be confused with beavers, minks or muskrats; however, beavers have large flat (rather than slender) tails, and minks and muskrats are much smaller.

NATURAL HISTORY As opportunistic feeders, river otters prey on a variety of aquatic and terrestrial organisms. In marine waters, they feed primarily on mid-sized, slower swimming fish that occur in nearshore areas—surfperch, sculpin, flatfish and spawned-out salmon. In freshwater areas, they prey on crayfish,

In the water, the river otter's low profile is difficult to spot.

TIMOTHY RANSOM

mussels and frogs. River otters are also major predators of diving birds and nesting birds and their young.

River otters do not build their own dens but rely instead on natural structures and cavities, the abandoned dens of other animals, thick shrubs and human

131

made structures—all usually located in isolated areas near some minimal source of fresh water.

Female otters generally breed at two or three years of age and give birth to between one and four young in spring every one or two years. They mate again shortly after the young are born but do not give birth until about eleven months later. After mating, there is a delay of about eight months before the fertilized egg is implanted and the fetus begins to develop. The otter pups are weaned after about five months, although they may stay with their mother for longer. River otters can be expected to live for ten to fifteen years.

River otters are generally more social than most other members of the weasel family. The primary social unit consists of the mother and her immature offspring. Sometimes more than one mother with pups will join together for a time; probably these mothers are closely related. Adult males are not usually found in company with the females, except during breeding season in late spring and early summer. The adult male and the

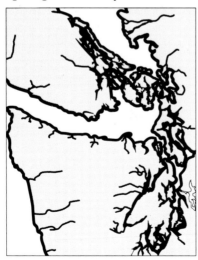

River Otter Distribution

Although difficult to observe in natural settings, river otters are often conspicuous on docks. TIMOTHY RANSOM

juvenile otters that have left their mother are usually solitary, although siblings may stick together for a while after they have been separated from their mothers. Additionally, in the San Juan Islands, some preliminary research suggests that males will occasionally band together to form bachelor groups of up to ten or fifteen individuals.

LOCAL DISTRIBUTION River otters occur widely throughout Greater Puget Sound, particularly around undeveloped streams and estuaries and along the beaches of the San Juan and Canadian Gulf Islands. Their population numbers in this region are unknown. About 500 river otters are trapped commercially every year in western Washington, with the highest numbers trapped in Clallam, Lewis, Pierce and Grays Harbor Counties. The trapping data show that river otters may

133

be depleted in some years, but in the inland waters of Greater Puget Sound more sightings now suggest that they may be increasing in this region.

HOW TO OBSERVE River otters can best be seen in estuary areas or close to shore in marine waters. They are most easily spotted when they climb out of the water onto docks, floats or exposed rocks and ledges to feed and play. At locations where they habitually crawl out of the water, they often leave behind crusty compact scats (dog-sized), usually containing fish and shellfish bones. The fresh scat is often dank and slimy. If you spot these scats, keep an eye out for river otters. From a high vantage point—such as a hillside or cliff at the water's edge—you may be able to see them hunt in shallow water, darting about after fish with remarkable speed and agility. River otters, although they keep a watchful eye out for humans, will often go about their normal activities if they are not threatened or if they are habituated to constant human presence, such as occurs around a marina.

134

C. J. CASSON/SEATTLE AQUARIUM

SEA OTTER

Enhydra lutris

During a boat survey for marine mammals near Neah Bay, Washington, in October of 1986, John Calambokidis caught a brief glimpse of a small animal on the edge of a dense kelp bed. It was too small to be a sea lion or a harbor seal, and its round light-colored head was shaped differently from that of a river otter. Though he suspected it to be a sea otter, he was very skeptical because of the rarity of this species in Greater Puget Sound. However, a subsequent survey and photographs

135

proved that it was indeed a sea otter—a male, probably exploring new territory. Alhough still a rare visitor to Greater Puget Sound, the sea otter has made a surprising comeback on Washington's outer coast, after its elimination there during the 18th and 19th centuries.

IDENTIFICATION The sea otter weighs up to 100 pounds and, at up to 5 feet in length, is the largest of the mustelid or weasel family. Its body is brown, except for the head, which may be light gray in color. It is covered with extremely dense fur that contains trapped air, thus providing great bouyancy. The ears and eyes are small, and the teeth are rounded or flattened. The tail is fairly short and stocky—especially in comparison to the more slender tail of the river otter—and the feet are webbed and flipper-like. The sea otter also often swims, rests and feeds on its back.

One must be careful not to mistake a sea otter for the far more common river otter. The sea otter differs from its cousin by its much larger size, grayish face, stockier, shorter tail (only one-quarter of the overall length) and a tendency to swim and eat on its back. In addition, the sea otter rarely crawls out of the water, as is common behavior for the river otter. The air trapped in its dense fur also makes it more buoyant than the river otter or any other marine mammal.

NATURAL HISTORY Sea otters were decimated by commercial hunters who sought and sold its fine fur during the 18th and 19th centuries. By the time the species was protected, only a few animals remained in remote or inaccessible portions of its range—in the western Aleutian Islands, along the Alaska Peninsula and along the central California coast. Populations in these areas have increased since protection, aided by a successful program to transplant otters to some other portions of their previous range. The most dramatic return has occurred in Alaska, where the sea otter population now surpasses 100,000.

The sea otter is a relatively voracious feeder, consuming about twenty percent of its body weight each day. Its favored foods are fish, sea urchins, shellfish and other easily caught marine organisms that inhabit shallow coastal waters. Often it brings its prey to the surface and consumes it while floating or swimming on its back. The sea otter has also developed a tool-using method for opening shellfish that cannot be crushed by its teeth: a rock carried on the chest is used as an anvil against which it crushes shellfish and thus gains access to the meat inside.

Sea otter predation on shellfish, particularly abalone and crab, has made repopulation of this species unwelcome in many areas. Increasing conflicts and controversy surround this species in California and in parts of Alaska where commercial fishermen have been negatively affected.

LOCAL DISTRIBUTION Sea otters used to be abundant

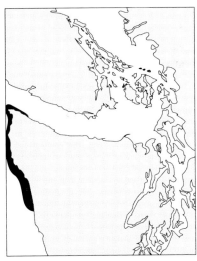

Sea Otter Distribution

137

on Washington's outer coast. They were common when the white man first arrived in the area, and their bones have been recovered from historical native village sites. The entire population was wiped out, however, by hunting in the 18th and 19th centuries. Between 1965 and 1972, sea otters were transplanted to southeast Alaska, British Columbia, Washington and Oregon, in an effort to re-establish the species to its former range. In Washington, the first transplant in 1969 apparently failed and most of the animals died, but a transplant of thirty animals in 1970 was successful. Today, after an apparent initial decline in numbers, sea otters have been increasing on the Washington outer coast. There are now about 100 animals concentrated at Cape Alava, Cape Johnson and Destruction Island.

The sea otter is not usually seen in the Greater Puget Sound area. In Washington State, observation of this animal in the wild is limited to the areas mentioned above. Because only a few have been confirmed for the inland waters, extreme caution must be used to ensure that sightings are not of river otters. Of course, if sea otter populations continue to increase, their range may expand, leading to more frequent sightings in the future.

HOW TO OBSERVE Sea otters are best observed from land with a spotting scope or binoculars. Those in Washington are extremely wary of approach by vessels. Scan areas in and near kelp beds—the most productive habitats in which to find these marine mammals.

MARINE MAMMAL
CONSERVATION

During this century, our perception of marine mammals and our relationships to them have changed dramatically. Until fifteen to twenty years ago, marine
mammals were still subject to heavy commercial exploitation throughout the world, but today, although
hunting continues in some places, marine mammals are
legally protected in the United States and Canada, with
only a few exceptions. Our relationship to marine
mammals has, it seems, gone through three phases—
the first, a period of subsistence whaling and sealing by
native cultures; the second, an era of overexploitation   139

by commercial whalers and sealers; and the third, a time of legal protection in which more subtle and indirect threats to these animals still exist. Here in the Pacific Northwest, we have experienced all of these phases.

Early native Americans in the Pacific Northwest, some of them using ingenious and daring methods, hunted marine mammals. In Hood Canal, the Skokomish hunted harbor seals in the marshes at high tide by burying sharp stakes just below water level and then scaring the seals so that they would impale themselves as they leaped into the water. Seals and sea lions were also hunted by the Lummi and the Samish in the Greater Puget Sound area. Probably the most proficient were the Makah living near Neah Bay and Cape Flattery and the Nootka living along the outer coast of Vancouver Island. Both of these groups hunted seals, sea lions, sea otters, porpoises and whales. They killed seals and sea lions on their land haul outs and northern fur seals at sea, often far offshore. In eight-man dugout canoes, they also pursued and harpooned gray whales and humpback whales.

The Indians impact on marine mammals was not significant. These early hunters were not very numerous, and their techniques, although effective, did not allow large numbers of animals to be killed. However, the "more civilized" era of commercial whaling and sealing that eventually followed was a different—and ugly—story. For their oil, baleen and fur, marine mammals were hunted during the 18th and 19th centuries in an unrelenting pattern of overexploitation that continued until the animals reached a point of "economic extinction"—a point at which so few animals were left that it was no longer profitable to hunt them. Species after species was driven to the brink of extinction, while protection or concern for their management were either never invoked or done so only after hunting was no longer profitable.

In the Pacific Northwest, shore-based whaling was conducted early in this century from stations at Bay City, Washington, along the west coast of Vancouver Island and in Georgia Strait. These stations operated with the aid of catcher-boats that ventured out to find and kill whales and then towed them back to shore for processing. Between 1911 and 1925, the Bay City station processed about 2,698 whales—most of them humpback and fin whales. On the outer coast of Vancouver Island, stations at Kyuquot and Sechart processed over 4,500 whales between 1905 and 1925, and a third station at Coal Harbour landed 10,317 whales between 1948 and 1967. The major species taken off Vancouver Island were fin, sperm, sei and humpback whales, with blue whales a minor part of the catch. In Georgia Strait, humpback whales were the major quarry, with whaling stations operating out of Hornby Island from 1866 to 1873 and out of Nanaimo from 1905 to 1908.

Also during the early part of this century, pinnipeds—primarily the harbor seal and the northern sea lion—were regarded as competitors with humans for fish. Between 1920 and 1960, a Washington State Department of Fisheries bounty system claimed an estimated 20,000 pinnipeds, paying enough for them that many people could make a living as hunters. Marine mammals during these years were regarded as vermin—their haul out areas were dynamited, and they were chased, shot and even strafed for target practice by military aircraft. Reflecting the attitude toward seals during this time is an article entitled "Varmint Hunting" in *Washington Outdoors* (1946):

"The season on these (seals) runs twelve months and   141

there is no limit . . . a person gets . . . the satisfaction of ridding the woods and waters of our state from a detrimental object plus the pleasure of some very good target shooting."

Somehow most marine mammal species recovered from the years of overexploitation. The California gray whale and many of the pinniped species are good examples. Others, like the blue whale and the right whale, have shown either no recovery or only imperceptibly slow improvement since they were protected.

Now within a few short years, the public's perception and the legal status of marine mammals have changed dramatically, both in the United States and Canada and, to a lesser extent, worldwide. After centuries of blatant overkill and being hunted as a scapegoat for declines in fish, marine mammals have become a *cause celebre*. The passage of the United States Marine Mammal Protection Act of 1972 is the most dramatic legal representation of this new attitude. Nonetheless, neither changes in attitude nor protective legislation have ended the threat to these creatures. In this third stage, the threats are less obvious but every bit as real: marine pollution, habitat destruction, conflicts with fisheries and human disturbance are all affecting marine mammals.

Today fishermen and marine mammals are once again in conflict. As the United States Marine Mammal Protection Act has succeeded in rejuvenating pinniped populations, it has also revived the fisherman's old complaints, some of which have proven incorrect or exaggerated. Pinniped predation on free-swimming salmon, for example, has been found to be relatively minor in all but a few isolated situations. However, predation on already-netted or hooked salmon and the damage to fishing gear that may result are significant. This damage is not always small; it can sometimes have

142

a dramatic financial impact on individual fishermen, especially when fish catches are already low.

In their interactions with fishing activities, marine mammals are often the victims. They are shot by fishermen guarding their gear; this is legal if the seal or sea lion is threatening or damaging property, and the fisherman has a permit. Sometimes they drown by becoming entangled in fishing gear. These incidents are increasingly common and are the leading causes of pinniped deaths in many areas. Thousands of marine mammals, both cetaceans and pinnipeds, are killed every year in purse-seining and deep-sea net fisheries. Most dramatic is the case of the northern fur seal as it feeds and migrates along the Washington and British Columbia coasts. This species has been declining since the mid-1970s at about six percent per year and is now at less than half of its historical numbers—probably because of entanglement in discarded pieces of netting and other fishing-related debris. In Greater Puget Sound, the primary cause of death in adult and subadult harbor seals is human-caused—from shooting and entanglement; gray whales that remain in the inland waters all summer are occasionally killed through entanglement in set nets near shore; and harbor and Dall's porpoises are frequently caught and killed in gill nets.

Pollution has also become a growing problem for marine mammals. In the 1960s, scientists discovered that PCBs and DDT were accumulating in the environment. Marine mammals are highly susceptible to these chemicals because they feed high on the food chain where concentrations are greatest and often live in coastal areas where these poisons accumulate. In some areas of Greater Puget Sound, harbor seals have been found with some of the highest concentrations in the world. Premature and deformed births documented in

143

the early 1970s may have been caused by these chemicals. The concentrations have been so high here that it would have been poisonous to consume harbor seal blubber, as natives have done in the past and transient orcas do at present. Many questions remain unanswered about the impact of pollutants on orcas in Greater Puget Sound, and a few limited samples have indicated that these marine mammals carry even higher concentrations than harbor seals. Likewise little is known about the possible impact of pollutants on river otters and harbor porpoises, both species that may have already suffered pollution-related problems.

Although the positive changes in our attitude toward marine mammals will surely help to protect them, there are dangers in our new-found love for them. Whole industries have arisen to promote and take advantage of human curiosity about whales and dolphins, seals, sea lions and otters. Whale-watching cruises are now common on all coasts of the United States and Canada. Recreational boaters and kayakers visit pinniped haul out areas to get a close look at the "cute seals." Pods of orcas in the San Juan Islands are sometimes followed by small flotillas of interested boaters. Seals lying on beaches are often picked up by sympathetic members of the public, even before their health status is determined. All of these activities could threaten marine mammals, if they remain unchecked.

Along with our growing appreciation of these creatures, we need also to become more aware of the effects of our own activities on them. We must obey the laws that protect them and not approach them too closely. Negligent or intentional disturbance or harassment of most marine mammals is illegal in Canada and illegal for all marine mammals in the United States under the

144 United States Marine Mammal Protection Act. This

includes approaching hauled out pinnipeds so closely that they enter the water and pursuing cetaceans until they change behavior or direction. In the United States, it is also illegal to pick up or possess any portion of a dead or sick marine mammal.

As the limits to how much we can disturb the environment become more evident, it will be increasingly important to live in harmony and share resources with the marine mammals. Only if we treat these fascinating creatures with appreciation and respect—as this new era of awareness dictates—can we hope to preserve them for future generations.

WHALE-WATCHING GUIDELINES

Vessels: Should not approach marine mammals closer than 100 yards.
Should not separate mothers and offspring.
Should approach whales slowly from the side, travel parallel to them and at the same speed as the slowest animals.

Aircraft: Should not fly under 1000 feet over marine mammals.

Operators: Should not perform any action that substantially disrupts normal behavior patterns.

To report incidents of marine mammal harassment, record the violator's vessel name and ID number and report it:

In Washington State:
National Marine Fisheries Service: (206) 526-6133
In British Columbia:
Department of Fisheries and Oceans: (604) 666-3500   145

REPORTING STRANDED MARINE MAMMALS

It is illegal to remove or disturb any stranded marine mammal without a federal stranding permit. Any dead marine mammal on a beach or floating is considered to be stranded. Additionally, any living marine mammal out of its element is considered stranded. However, a seal or sea lion hauled out on a beach or rock is not necessarily stranded and may return to the sea on its own; such an animal must be watched for a while before being considered stranded.

The Northwest Marine Mammal Stranding Network is a volunteer effort of many agencies, institutions and individuals in the United States who are under federal permit to respond to strandings. Its members are authorized to rescue live marine mammals and collect scientific data from both live and dead strandings. In Canada, strandings are responded to by the Department of Fisheries and Oceans or interested museums and conservation organizations.

If you encounter a stranded marine mammal, do not touch it or disturb it. Instead record a description of the animal, its exact location and the time and the date it was seen. Then, as soon as possible, report this information to the proper authorities listed below.

To report cetacean sightings and marine mammal strandings in Washington State, call the State Patrol, the local police or the Whale Hotline, 1-800-562-8832.

In British Columbia, call the Department of Fisheries and Oceans, Radio Dispatch: (604) 666-3500 or the Whale Hotline, 1-800-334-8832.

INDIVIDUAL RESIDENT ORCAS IN GREATER PUGET SOUND

This catalog contains illustrations of the fins and saddle patches of the eighty-two resident orcas (killer whales) that currently inhabit the waters within a 200-mile radius of the San Juan Islands. They range, year-round, throughout Greater Puget Sound north to Campbell River, British Columbia; move west out the Strait of Juan de Fuca and along the coast, north at least to Tofino and south at least to La Push. How far offshore in the Pacific Ocean they actually travel is not known.

Extended family groups of whales that always travel together are called pods; at times, a pod may join with others, forming larger, multi-pod community groups. Using the   147 identification system developed by the Canadian biologist, Michael Bigg, each pod is assigned a letter designation, and each individual within the pod is given a number. In 1984 The Whale Museum developed a program to encourage public interest in the whales. Researchers named each animal and wrote biographies to indicate every orca's lineage. This approach has been helpful in increasing public awareness of marine mammals and other marine species.

Individual orcas are identified by the two parts of their bodies that are most prominent when they surface to breathe: the dorsal fin and the white marking just behind it called the saddle patch. The dorsal fins of many whales are marked with distinctive nicks, scars or tears, while saddle patches appear to be as unique to each individual as are our fingerprints. Adult male orcas have larger dorsal fins than do adult females and juveniles. If the height of a whale's fin is greater than its width at the base, then the animal is an adult male. All orcas whose dorsal fins are not noticeably taller than they are wide at the base are either adult females or juveniles. The tallest dorsal fin in the resident community of pods belongs to Ruffles (J-1); his is nearly six feet tall.

Within a pod, certain groups of individuals are consistently found together during most daily activities. Scientists believe these subgroups are family units within the pods which revolve around mothers and their offspring. No orca has been seen to leave its mother's subgroup, nor has any whale ever been known to gain membership in a pod subgroup other than by birth. Although specific fathers are unknown, scientists suspect that males mate with females from other pods within the community during multi-pod gatherings and then return to their mother's pod when mating is finished and/or the multi-pod groups split.

The following drawings are based on photographs collected over the last fourteen years by scientists from both Canada and the United States. Without this continuous cooperative effort, such accurate drawings would be impossible, as would the understanding of family relationships between the individual whales.

SUCIA'S SUBGROUP / J-POD

J-3 MERLIN *The Loner.*

Merlin, one of the three adult males in J-Pod, is known to be at least thirty years old because he was photographed as an adolescent during a Puget Sound capture in 1968 and as an adult in a capture in 1972. Both times, Merlin was released instead of being taken to an aquarium. He spent most of his time traveling with his mother, Sucia (J-7), until she died in 1984. Now Merlin is usually found by himself or with his young adolescent brother, Slick (J-16).

J-16 SLICK *Motherless Son.*

Slick is a young adolescent male member of J-Pod and the youngest son of Sucia (J-7) who died in 1984. Now Slick spends most of his time traveling on the periphery of the pod with his older brother Merlin (J-3). Slick was first photographed as a two year old in 1974, so he is now a teenager. His dorsal fin is now beginning to grow noticeably as he takes his place beside the other adult bulls of J-Pod.

149

J-2 GRANNY *The Matriarch.*
Granny may be the oldest female in J-Pod. First photographed in 1972 when she and others were captured in Puget Sound, she was released. She appeared to be an adult then but has not given birth in the last fourteen years. Researchers thus think she is very old and, based upon her pod associations, may be the mother of Sissy (J-12) and Ruffles (J-1).

J-1 RUFFLES *The Elder.*
Ruffles is probably the oldest male in J-Pod, and his 6-foot dorsal fin is the tallest in the resident pods. Based upon photographs dating back to 1974, scientists figure Ruffles is at least thirty years old. He spends much of his time with Granny (J-2), who is most likely his mother, his sister, Sissy (J-12), and her offspring. Ruffles received his name because of the wavy edge along the back of his dorsal fin.

J-12 SISSY *A New Grandmother.*
Sissy was first photographed as an adult with her one-year-old daughter, Samish (J-14) in 1974. She has had no other calves since 1973, so researchers estimate she is at least twenty-eight years old. In 1986 Sissy became a grandmother with the December birth of Capricorn (J-23) to Samish. Researchers believe Sissy's mother is Granny (J-2) and her brother is Ruffles (J-1).

J-14 SAMISH *Teen Mother.*

Samish, the newest mother in J-Pod, gave birth at age thirteen to her first calf, Capricorn (J-23), in December of 1986. Most new orca mothers in the resident pods give birth to their first calf at the age of fourteen to sixteen years. The birth of Capricorn makes Sissy (J-12) a grandmother and probably makes Granny (J-2) a great-grandmother and Ruffles (J-1) a great-uncle.

J-23 CAPRICORN *December's Child.*

Capricorn was born sometime between December 20th and 25th, 1986. The new calf and its mother, Samish (J-14), were photographed by Canadian researcher Michael Bigg on December 27, 1986. As Samish's first calf, Capricorn is Sissy's (J-12) first granddaughter; probably Granny's (J-2) first great-granddaughter; and Ruffles' (J-1) great-niece.

J-8 SPIEDEN *A Favorite Granny.*

Spieden is a very old female first photographed as an adult when captured in Puget Sound in 1968. She has never been documented with a calf of her own which suggests she is beyond calf-bearing years. Spieden's close association with Mama (J-4) and Ralph (J-6) suggests that they are her adult offspring. If true, Spieden would be at least in her late fifties and more likely sixties or seventies.

J-6 RALPH *The Babysitter.*

Ralph is considered the youngest adult bull in J-Pod, but scientists estimate he is at least twenty-eight years old. Based upon his usual associates, researchers believe he is either the son or brother of Mama (J-4) and thus either the son or grandson of Spieden (J-8). Ralph is known as the "babysitter" because he was once seen in the company of the calves and juveniles of J-Pod for more than four continuous hours.

J-4 MAMA *Always There When She's Needed.* Mama is an adult female who has given birth to more calves than any other female in J-Pod during the last decade. The mother of Blossom (J-11), Shachi (J-19), E.T. (J-21) who died in 1984 and J-15 who died in 1982, she often travels with Ralph (J-6) and Spieden (J-8) who helps care for her presumed grandchildren.

J-11 BLOSSOM *Mother's Helper.*
Blossom is thought to be around fifteen years old. Her mother is Mama (J-4), and her younger sibling is Shachi (J-19). Blossom used to have two additional younger siblings for whom she often babysat: J-15, a brother who died in 1982; and E.T. (J-21) who died in 1984. Researchers expect Blossom to have her first calf soon, making Spieden (J-8) a great-grandmother.

J-19 SHACHI *Japanese for Orca.*
Shachi, a juvenile who was born in the spring of 1979, is now Mama's (J-4's) youngest calf after the unfortunate disappearance of one-year-old E.T. (J-21) in 1984. Shachi spends most of its time with Mama, older sister Blossom (J-11), and granny Spieden (J-8), as well as the other J-Pod calves.

153

J-10 TAHOMA *Mother of Three.*

Tahoma, an adult female, is known to be at least twenty-seven years old from a capture photograph in 1972. Since then, she has given birth to three calves: Everett (J-18) in 1977, Ewok (J-20) in 1980 and Oreo (J-22) in 1985. It was believed that Neah (J-9), who disappeared in 1985-86, was the mother of Tahoma and Saratoga (J-5) because she was seen frequently with them

J-18 EVERETT *The Eldest Child.*

Everett, a juvenile member of J-Pod, was born in the early winter of 1977, the oldest offspring of Tahoma (J-10). S/he has two younger siblings, Ewok (J-20) and Oreo (J-22). Everett's grandmother was probably Neah (J-9) who disappeared in 1986, and his/her aunt is Saratoga (J-5). It is still too early to tell if this whale is male or female, but by the time Everett is thirteen years old, researchers should know from the size of its dorsal fin.

J-20 EWOK *The Trickster.*

Ewok, a young juvenile member of J-Pod, is Tahoma's (J-10) second youngest offspring, born in the winter-spring of 1979-80. In addition to its mother, Ewok spends much time traveling with his/her siblings, Everett (J-18) and Oreo (J-22).

J-22 OREO *Everybody's Sweetie.*
Oreo is a calf who was born during late November or early December of 1984. S/he is Tahoma's (J-10's) third offspring and has two older siblings, Everett and Ewok. Oreo spends most of his/her time with Tahoma but used to swim with grandma Neah (J-9) before she disappeared in 1986.

J-5 SARATOGA *Mother of a Princess.*
Saratoga, an adult female member of J-Pod first photographed during a Puget Sound capture in 1968, is known to be at least thirty years old and is probably much older. Saratoga has had two calves: J-13 who died in 1981 and Princess Angeline (J-17), born in the spring of 1977. Researchers suspect that Saratoga was the daughter of Neah (J-9) who presumably died in 1985-86. This would also make her the sister of Tahoma (J-10) and the aunt of Tahoma's three offspring.

J-17 PRINCESS ANGELINE *The Remaining Daughter.* Princess Angeline was born to Saratoga (J-5) in the early spring of 1977, and researchers named her after Chief Seattle's daughter. Her probable grandmother, Neah (J-9), disappeared in 1985-86 and her sister, J-13, disappeared in 1981. Other close relatives include her aunt Tahoma (J-10) and cousins Everett (J-18), Ewok (J-20) and Oreo (J-22).

155

K-POD / TUMWATER'S SUBGROUP

K-8 TUMWATER *Elder Lady.*
Tumwater is an adult female member of K-Pod, the probable mother of Sealth (K-5) and Sounder (K-3) and the grandmother of Leon (K-l4) and Opus (K-l6). She now appears to be beyond the calf-bearing years and so is probably a minimum of forty years old.

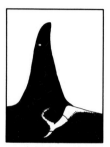 

K-5 SEALTH *The Oldest Bull.*
Sealth is an adult male member of K-Pod who is at least thirty-three years old. First photographed as an adult in a 1967 capture, his dorsal fin has a tilt to the right at the tip which makes him easy to recognize. Researchers suspect that Sealth is the son of Tumwater (K-8), the brother of Sounder (K-3) and the uncle of Leon (K-14) and Opus (K-16).

K-3 SOUNDER *Mother of Two.*

Sounder is an adult female member of K-Pod who has a juvenile son, Leon (K-14), and a calf of unknown sex, Opus (K-16). In 1975 she had another calf, K-15, who disappeared as a juvenile. Researchers suspect that Sounder is the daughter of Tumwater (K-8) and the sister of Sealth (K-5). Since Opus is at least her third calf, Sounder is at least thirty years old.

K-14 LEON *Becoming Bullish.*

Leon is a juvenile male member of K-Pod who has just begun to sprout a dorsal fin that is taller than his mother's. Born to Sounder (K-3) in 1977, he was only recognized as a male in 1986, and his name was changed from Leia. Leon has a younger sibling, Opus (K-16), and is often found traveling in the close company of his uncle, Sealth (K-5), and grandmother, Tumwater (K-8).

K-16 OPUS *A Bloom County Fan.*

Opus is a calf of unknown sex whose mother is Sounder (K-3) and older brother is Leon (K-14). This calf is often found playing around its new younger cousins, Spock (K-20) and Cappuccino (K-21). Opus also spends much time with its grandmother, Tumwater (K-8), and good old Uncle Sealth (K-5).

157

K-4 MORGAN *Sea Witch.*
Morgan is an adult member of K-Pod first documented in 1974 with her two-year-old daughter, Sequim (K-12). In 1987 Sequim gave birth to her first calf, Sekiu (K-22), making Morgan a grand-mother. It is not clear who Morgan's other close relatives are, though she may be the sister of Taku (K-1).

K-12 SEQUIM *Teeny Bopper.*
Sequim is a teenage female member of K-Pod who was born in 1972 to Morgan (K-4) and gave birth to her first calf, Sekiu (K-22), in 1987 at the age of 15. She has no other close relatives that re-searchers can discern, except a possible uncle, Taku (K-1).

K-22 SEKIU *The Youngest Calf.*
Sekiu was born in the spring of 1987 to Sequim (K-12). Sekiu is Sequim's first calf and Morgan's (K-4) first grandchild. Sekiu is still too young to discern if it is male or female.

K-1 TAKU *The Top Knotch Bull.*
Taku is an adult male member of K-Pod who was first photographed in 1973 when he was captured in British Colum-bia. He had two triangular notches cut into his dorsal fin so that researchers could easily recognize him after release. Based on past photographs, Taku's age is estimated to be around thirty-two years. His association with other whales suggests that he is the son of K-6, a female who disappeared in 1974, and possibly the brother of Morgan (K-4) or Lummi (K-7).

K-7 LUMMI *The Great-Grandmother.*
Lummi is an adult female member of K-Pod named after a Northwest tribe of native Americans who live in and around the San Juan Islands. Her daughter is probably Georgia (K-11), her grandaughter, Skagit (K-13), and her great-grandchild, Spock (K-20).

K-11 GEORGIA *Straight-Laced Lady.*
Georgia is an adult female member of K-Pod who was named after the Strait of Georgia. She is probably the daughter of Lummi (K-7), the mother of Skagit (K-13) and the grandmother of Spock (K-20).

K-13 SKAGIT *New Mother.*
Skagit is a young adult female member of K-Pod who gave birth to her first calf, Spock (K-20), in 1986 at the age of fourteen. Her mother is Georgia (K-11), and her grandmother is probably Lummi (K-7).

K-20 SPOCK *A Whale With a Mission.*
Spock was born sometime in the winter-spring of 1986, the first calf of Skagit (K-13). Skagit was only thirteen years old when Spock was born, though most first mothers are between fourteen and sixteen years old. The birth of Spock makes Georgia (K-11) a grandmother, and probably makes Lummi (K-7) a great-grandmother. It is not yet known if Spock is male or female, but the name can be used for either sex on the fictional planet of Vulcan.

159

K-POD/KISKA'S SUBGROUP

K-18 KISKA *A Joiner.*
Kiska, an adult female of K-Pod has had four offspring since 1974. That year she traveled with a nine-year-old daughter, Raggedy (K-40); a six-year-old son, Pacheena (K-17); and a two-year-old calf (K-46) who disappeared in 1981. In 1986 Kiska had Cappucino (K-21), who will probably be her last calf because she is about thirty-six years old.

K-21 CAPPUCINO *Always Ready to Go.*
Cappucino was born during the winter-spring of l986 and is at least the fourth calf of Kiska (K-18), formerly L-18. Cappy's brother is Pacheena (K-17) and his/her sister is Raggedy (K-40).

K-17 PACHEENA *Twilighting Teenager.*
Pacheena is a young adult male of K-Pod who was a late bloomer, his dorsal fin slowly increasing in size over recent years. He now appears to be reaching physical maturity. His mother is Kiska (K-18), and his sister is Raggedy (K-40). In 1986 he gained a baby sibling, Cappucino (K-21), with whom he is very gentle and protective.

K-40 RAGGEDY *A Tattered Lady.*
Raggedy, named for the tattered condition of her dorsal fin, is a young female of K-Pod. She often helps her mother, Kiska (K-18), take care of her new sibling, Cappucino (K-21). She also used to help care for K-46 who disappeared in l981, and her younger brother, Pacheena (K-l7). Raggedy has never had a calf, although she is believed to be about twenty-two years old.

L-2 GRACE *Mother of Two.*
Grace is an adult female member of L-Pod first photographed in 1974 as an adult without a calf. In 1975 she gave birth to Orcan (L-39), and a decade later she gave birth to Splash (L-67). Grace must be at least twenty-six years old and is probably much older.

L-39 ORCAN *Child of Grace.*
Orcan is a young adult male member of L-Pod who was first identified as a newborn in 1975 with his mother Grace (L-2). A decade later, Grace gave birth to a second calf, Splash (L-67), who is now Orcan's only sibling. Orcan is just now showing definite signs of growing the large dorsal fin characteristic of adult bulls.

L-67 SPLASH *Child of Grace.*
Splash is a juvenile member of L-Pod, whose sex is not yet known. First photographed in 1985 as the newborn calf of Grace (L-2), Splash has an older brother, Orcan (L-39), who is usually found traveling with Splash and Grace.

161

L-8 SUBPOD/ANKH'S SUBGROUP

L-21 ANKH *Single Mother.*
Ankh is an adult female member of L-Pod who was first photographed in 1974 as an adult with a brand new calf, Marina (L-47). Later, in 1978, she was photographed with a second calf, Flash (L-48), but Flash disappeared at the age of five in 1983. No other whales appear to have significantly close relations with Ankh and Marina.

L-47 MARINA *Only Child.*
Marina is a young adult female member of L-Pod first photographed in 1974 as Ankh's (L-2l) newborn calf. She used to have a younger sibling, Flash (L-48), who was born in 1978 and disappeared in 1983. Ankh has not had any more calves since then, making Marina an only child.

162

L-26 BABA *Traveling Mother.*

Baba is an adult female member of L-Pod, first photographed in 1974 with her daughter, Rascal (L-60), who was then only one year old. In 1979, six years later, Baba gave birth to a second calf, Salish (L-52), who died in 1983. Then, in 1986, Baba gave birth to a third calf, Hugo (L-71). Researchers suspect that Baba must now be at least twenty-eight years old.

L-60 RASCAL *Big Sister.*

Rascal is an adolescent female member of L-Pod, first photographed in 1974 as a one or two year old. Her mother is Baba (L-26). Rascal was an only child up until 1980 when Baba gave birth to Salish (L-52), and then she became an only child again when Salish died in 1983. Rascal is expected to have her first calf soon.

L-71 HUGO *Big Sister's Shadow.*

Hugo was first photographed in June 1986 off Race Rocks in the Strait of Juan de Fuca by International Cetacean Watch researchers. At least the third offspring of Baba (L-26), Hugo has an older sister, Rascal (L-60), who is expected to have her first calf soon. Hugo's sibling, Salish (L-52), disappeared in 1983.

L-8 SUBPOD/SONAR'S SUBGROUP

L-4 SONAR *Proud Grandmother.*
Sonar is an adult female member of L-Pod, first photographed in 1974 with a one-year-old calf, Astral (L-61). In 1977 she had another calf, Nugget (L-55). Based upon her associations, she is also believed to be the mother of the adult female, Ophelia (L-27), who gave birth to her first calf (Sonar's first grandchild), Cetus (L-62), in 1980. In 1985 Sonar gained a second grandchild, Elwah (L-68), through Ophelia (L-27) .

L-61 ASTRAL *Young Man of the Family.*
Astral is an adolescent male member of L-Pod first photographed in 1974 as a one-year-old calf traveling with his mother, Sonar (L-4). Astral has one older sister, Ophelia (L-27), and another older sibling, Nugget (L-55). He is now the only adult bull in his maternal family group.

L-55 NUGGET *Ripe for Life.*
Nugget is a juvenile member of L-Pod of undetermined sex. First photographed in 1977 as the newborn calf of Sonar (L-4), Nugget's probable older brother and sister are Astral (L-61) and Ophelia (L-27). Older sister Ophelia has two calves of her own and is estimated to be at least twenty-one years old. It is expected that Nugget will be the last calf old Sonar will have.

L-27 OPHELIA *Mother of Two.*

Ophelia is an adult female member of L-Pod, first photographed in 1974 as an eight-year-old juvenile traveling with her mother, Sonar (L-4), and newborn brother, Astral (L-61). In 1980, at the age of fourteen, Ophelia gave birth to her first calf, Cetus (L-62), and in 1985 she gave birth to her second calf, Elwah (L-68). Ophelia is now in her early twenties.

L-62 CETUS *The Whale.*

Cetus is a juvenile member of L-Pod whose sex is not yet known. Cetus was photographed in 1980 as the newborn first calf of Ophelia (L-27). Cetus' grandmother is Sonar (L-4), and his/her sibling is Elwah (L-68). They are always found traveling with Uncle Astral (L-61) and young Nugget (L-55).

L-68 ELWAH *Newest Addition.*

Elwah is a calf of L-Pod whose sex has not yet been determined. First photographed in 1985 as the newborn calf of Ophelia (L-27), Elwah is also often found traveling with Granny Sonar (L-4), Uncle Astral (L-61) and Aunt or Uncle Nugget (L-55).

165

L-8 SUBPOD/KIMO'S SUBGROUP

L-7 CANUCK *Surviving Matriarch.*
Canuck was first photographed in 1974, traveling in the close company of her probable mother, Kimo (L-37), her young sister, Jelly Roll (L-43), and her adult brother, or possible son, L-l6. Canuck gave birth to Lulu (L-53) in 1977 and Mowgli (L-76) in 1987. Her adult brother or son, L-16, disappeared a year later. Then, during the winter of 1984-85, her mother disappeared, so Canuck is now the oldest surviving female in her family.

L-53 LULU *An Only Cousin.*
Lulu is a juvenile member of L-Pod who was first photographed in l977 as Canuck's (L-7) newborn calf. Lulu has no other siblings, and his/her apparent grandmother, Kimo (L-37), disappeared during the winter of l984-85. In 1987 Lulu got a new baby sibling, Mowgli (L-76). Lulu is still too young to tell if s/he is male or female. Canuck and Lulu spend most of their time traveling with Aunt Jelly Roll (L-43) and Lulu's young cousin, Racer (L-72).

L-76 MOWGLI *A New Spirit in the Pod.*
Mowgli is a calf born sometime during the winter-spring of 1986-1987 and is the second calf of Canuck (L-7), joining older sibling, Lulu (L-53). Canuck, Lulu and Mowgli spend most of their time traveling with aunt Jelly Roll (L-43) and young cousin Racer (L-72).

L-43 JELLY ROLL *New Mother on Her Own.* Jelly Roll is an adult female member of L-Pod, first photographed in 1974 as a two year old traveling with her mother, Kimo (L-37). Canuck (L-7) is thought to be her older sister. During the winter of 1984-85, Jelly Roll's mother, Kimo, disappeared, leaving her in the company of her sister and niece, Lulu (L-53). Then, in l986 at the age of fourteen, Jelly Roll gave birth to her first calf, Racer (L-72).

L-72 RACER *Always First To Get There.* Canadian researchers first photo-graphed this orca off Race Rocks in June 1987—hence his/her name. Racer is the first calf of Jelly Roll (L-43), who was sixteen years old at the time. Ever since Jelly Roll's mother, Kimo (L-37), died in 1984, Racer has spent most of her time traveling with Canuck (L-7) and her offspring, Lulu (L-53), in L-8 sub-pod. Researchers suspect that Canuck is Jelly Roll's older sister, and that is why they spend so much time together.

167

L-8 SUBPOD/HOPI'S SUBGROUP

L-9 HOPI *Wise Old Matriarch.*
Hopi was first photographed in 1974 as an adult female, with her close companion, Tanya (L-5), who appeared to be her juvenile calf. Hopi has not been documented with a calf since, but often babysits the calves of Oriana (L-3) and Tanya (L-5). Hopi is probably the more than sixty-year-old grandmother of this subgroup.

L-3 ORIANA *Island Traveler.*
Oriana is an adult female of L-Pod. Believed to be the daughter of Hopi (L-9), the sister of Tanya (L-5) and the mother of Chinook (L-33), she was first photographed in 1974 traveling with Hopi, Chinook and a new calf, Nootka (L-51). In 1986 she gave birth to Saanich (L-74).

L-33 CHINOOK *The Bull of the Family.*
Chinook was first photographed in 1974 as an adolescent male traveling with Oriana (L-3), his probable mother; his newborn sister, Nootka (L-51); and his probable grandmother, Hopi (L-9). He is now in his early twenties and the only full grown bull in his subgroup.

L-51 NOOTKA *Northwest Native.*
Nootka is a young adult female of L-Pod documented in 1974 as Oriana's (L-3) new calf. Her grandmother appears to be Hopi (L-9), and her brother is probably Chinook (L-33). Nootka also has a baby sibling, Saanich (L-74). Nootka's family is the largest maternal group in the resident community of pods.

L-74 SAANICH *Baby of the Family.*
Saanich is the third offspring of Oriana (L-3) and is named after the peninsula and bay just north of Victoria, B.C. Born during the winter/spring of 1985-86, she has an older sister, Nootka (L-51), and an older brother, Chinook (L-33). They spend most of their time traveling with Grandma Hopi (L-9), Tanya and her kids.

L-5 TANYA *Wandering Female.*
Tanya's travels have been closely watched since 1974 when she was first photographed in the close company of her probable mother, Hopi (L-9), and sister, Oriana (L-3). Tanya is considered a young female in her early twenties, having given birth to what appears to be her first calf, Sparky (L-58), in 1980. In 1986 she gave birth to Flash (L-73).

L-73 FLASH *Newest Grandchild.*
Flash was born sometime during the winter of 1985-86 and is the second offspring of Tanya (L-5). This whale also has an older sibling, Sparky (L-58). Along with Tanya and Sparky, Flash is a member of L-8 sub-pod. With the birth of Flash, Hopi is now a grandmother five times over.

L-8 SUBPOD/OCEAN SUN'S SUBGROUP

L-25 OCEAN SUN *Westward Bound.*
Ocean Sun is an adult female member of L-Pod, first photographed in 1974 traveling with Tsunami (L-23) and Tsunami's male calf, Cordy (L-14). Tsunami disappeared during the winter of 1981-82, and, ever since, Cordy has traveled primarily with Ocean Sun. She has never been seen with a young calf of her own, so researchers suspect that she is a very old female. She was possibly the mother of Tsunami and is thus the grandmother of Cordy. Perhaps this is why Ocean Sun and Cordy travel together so often.

L-14 CORDY *Raised By Grandmother.*
Cordy is a young adolescent male member of L-Pod, first photographed as a two-year-old calf traveling with his mother, Tsunami (L-23). Tsunami disappeared and presumably died in 1982, and now Cordy travels closely with Ocean Sun (L-25), his presumed grandmother, who was also his primary babysitter during childhood.

L-45 ASTERIX *Still Has Faith.*

Asterix is an adult female member of L-Pod who was first documented in 1974 with her mother, Mata Hari (L-66). She and her mother were nearly identical in appearance, and it was not until 1985 that researchers were sure they were two different individuals. In 1977 Asterix gave birth to a male calf, Faith (L-57).

L-57 FAITH *He's Hangin' In.*

Faith is an adolescent male member of L-Pod who was first photographed in 1977 as Asterix's (L-45) newborn calf. In 1986 he began to show the early signs of growing the large dorsal fin that is characteristic of bulls. Also in 1986, Faith lost his grandmother, Mata Hari (L-66), who washed up dead near Port Alberni on Vancouver Island.

171

L-10 SUBPOD/OKUM

L-10 OKUM *The Sea Wolf.*
Okum is an adult male member of L-Pod, first photographed in 1974 as a nearly full grown adult, so researchers estimate he is around thirty years old. L-10 does not have a close enough association with any one whale to guess who his mother might be or whether she is even alive. However, he is regularly seen with members of Alexis' (L-12) subgroup and Misky's (L-28) subgroup. Perhaps Alexis and Misky are his older sisters or maternal aunts.

L-12 ALEXIS *Mozart's Grandmother.*

Alexis is an adult female member of L-Pod who was first photographed in 1974 as an old adult. Never seen with a calf of her own, Alexis has close associations with Squirty (L-11) and her calves, which suggests she is an immediate member of the family. Scientists believe she is Squirty's mother and, thus, grandmother to Mega (L-41) and Mozart (L-42).

L-11 SQUIRTY *Mozart's Mother.*

Squirty is an adult female member of L-Pod who was first photographed in l974 as the mother of the calf Mozart (L-42). Old Alexis (L-12) often babysits for Squirty's calves and is believed to be Squirty's mother. In 1977 Squirty gave birth to her second calf, Mega (L-41).

L-42 MOZART *Whale of Note.*

Mozart is a young adolescent male member of L-Pod who was first photographed as a one year old in 1974 , while traveling with his mother, Squirty (L-11), and probable grandmother, Alexis (L-12). In 1977 he was joined by a younger brother, Mega (L-41).

L-41 MEGA *Spring Child.*

Mega is a juvenile male member of L-Pod who is just beginning to show the dorsal fin growth characteristic of an adult bull. He was first photographed as a newborn in 1977, traveling with his mother, Squirty (L-11), older brother, Mozart (L-42), and probable grandmother, Alexis (L-12).

173

L-10 SUBPOD/MISKY'S SUBGROUP

L-28 MISKY *The Great Grandmother.*
Misky was first photographed as an adult in 1974 and has never been seen with a young calf of her own. Researchers suspect she is Olympia's (L-32) mother. This would make Misky a grandmother four times over and a great-grandmother with the birth of Panda (L-75) to her granddaughter, Spirit (L-22), in 1986. It is believed that Misky is one of the oldest orcas around, perhaps more than sixty years old.

L-32 OLYMPIA *Grandmother and Mother of Twins.* Olympia was first photographed in 1974 as an adult female with a juvenile, Spirit (L-22), a new born calf, Leo (L-44) and a probable adolescent son, Dylan (L-38). She has since given birth to Disney (L-56) who died in 1982 and to twins, Scotia (L-63) and Sumner (L-69) in 1984. Unfortunately, Sumner died in 1986, but during the same year Spirit gave birth to her first calf, Panda (L-75), making Olympia a confirmed grandmother.

L-38 DYLAN *Young and Restless.*
Dylan is a young adult male member of L-Pod. He was first photographed in 1974, traveling in close association with Olympia (L-32), his presumed mother, and Spirit (L-22) and Leo (L-44), his probable siblings. Since 1974 he has gained four additional siblings, but two of them, Disney (L-56) and Sumner (L-69), disappeared at very young ages and are probably dead. Dylan is now estimated to be in his early twenties.

174

L-44 LEO *The Harmonizer.*
Leo is a young adult male of L-Pod, first photographed in 1974 as Olympia's (L-32) new calf. As a teenager, Leo is showing definite signs of becoming a bull. The adult bull, Dylan (L-38), appears to be Leo's older brother, and Spirit (L-22), his older sister. Leo also has a younger sibling, Scotia (L-63).

L-63 SCOTIA *Child of the Northern Isles.*
Scotia is a young member of L-Pod whose sex has not yet been determined. Scotia was first photographed in 1984 as the newborn calf of Olympia (L-32). Scotia's older siblings are Leo (L-44), Spirit (L-22) and Dylan (L-38).

L-22 SPIRIT *The Changer.*
Spirit is a young adult female of L-Pod first photographed in 1974 as the four-year-old calf of Olympia (L-32). In 1986, at the age of 16, Spirit gave birth to her first calf, Panda (L-75). Previously, researchers had thought that Spirit was the mother of Sumner (L-69) because she took primary care of the calf, but when Spirit gave birth to Panda, it became obvious that this was not true.

L-75 PANDA *First Born.*
Panda is the first offspring of Spirit (L-22). In 1986 scientists thought Sumner (L-69) was Spirit's first calf because Sumner spent so much time traveling closely with Spirit. However, it appears that Spirit's mother, Olympia (L-32), gave birth to twins in the winter of 1984-85. Now we know that Spirit was already pregnant with Panda at the time Sumner was born.

L-35 SUBPOD/VICTORIA'S SUBGROUP

L-35 VICTORIA *Matriarchal Queen.*
Victoria is an adult female member of L-Pod who was first documented in 1974 as an adult with a one-year-old calf, Shala (L-50). In 1977 she gave birth to Ino (L-54) who is now a budding adolescent bull, and in 1984 she gave birth to Aquarius (L-65). Except for Oskar (L-1), Victoria and her offspring stay to themselves and often travel separately from the rest of L-Pod. Victoria's relationship to Oscar is unknown: she may be either his mother or sister.

L-1 OSKAR *Queen Victoria's Knight.*
Oscar is an adult male member of L-Pod who is estimated to be around thirty years old. First photographed in 1974 as an adult, it is not known who Oscar's mother is, but he does spend a great deal of time traveling with Victoria (L-35) and her calves. He could be the son of Victoria but is more likely her brother, judging from the ages of Victoria's offspring, Shala (L-50), Ino (L-54) and Aquarius (L-65).

L-50 SHALA *Teen Angel.*

Shala is a young adult male member of L-Pod. He was first photographed in 1974 as the one-year-old calf of Victoria (L-35). Shala is either the nephew or the younger brother of Oscar. His younger siblings are Ino (L-54) and Aquarius (L-65). As a teenager, Shala is now starting to show the large dorsal fin characteristic of bulls.

L-54 INO *The Kid.*

Ino is a juvenile member of L-Pod, and it is not yet clear if this whale is male or female. Ino was first photographed in 1977 as a newborn calf with its mother, Victoria (L-35). Ino's older brother is Shala (L-50), and his younger sibling is Aquarius (L-65). Together with Uncle Oskar (L-1), Ino and his family often travel separately from the rest of L-Pod.

L-65 AQUARIUS *Child of the New Age.*

Aquarius is a young member of L-Pod whose gender is not yet known. This whale was first photographed in 1984 as Victoria's (L-35) newborn calf. Aquarius has two older siblings, Ino (L-54) and Shala (L-50). Aquarius' family, including Uncle Oskar (L-1), often travels separately from the rest of L-Pod.

177

INDIVIDUAL MINKE WHALES IN THE SAN JUAN ISLANDS

Twenty-eight individual minke whales have been identified in the San Juan Islands. These individuals are recognized by the shape and sometimes the color of the dorsal fin, the distribution of small circular scars on the body and the pattern of pale pigmentation on the sides. This minke whale catalog contains illustrations of all twenty-eight dorsal fins in side profile, along with some information about each whale. Examples of the small scars and the pale swaths of pigmentation can be found in the photos accompanying the minke whale species account which begins on page 77.

Almost half of the minkes in the San Juans can be identified from their dorsal fins alone because they are very distinctive. These whales are presented first in the catalog. The remaining whales have less distinctive fins and are assigned to one of three categories: fins with long curves, fins with short curves and triangular fins. Minkes within these categories are distinguished by the scars and pigmentation on their sides.

179

The dorsal fin drawings show the profile of the fin from both right and left sides in broadside view. (If seen from any other angle, the profile can look very different.) Nicks or other irregularities in the profile are highlighted by a black line, and any unusual pale pigmentation is indicated by stippling. The fin of a few minke whales bends to one side or the other, and this is noted in the description.

Because minke whales usually surface too rapidly to allow careful observation, it is almost always necessary to have a photograph for certain identification. Although United States federal law prohibits approaching any whale closer than 100 yards without a research permit, minke whales occasionally swim up to a boat and can be photographed at close range without violation of the law.

Photographs of local minkes can help us learn more about these whales, especially when records are kept of when and approximately where the animal was seen. The Whale Museum gratefully accepts prints, slides or negatives of minke whales and will copy and return originals if requested. Mail to the following address:

The Whale Museum-Minke Project
Post Office Box 945
Friday Harbor, Washington 98250

The information on individual minke whales presented here is taken from research conducted by Eleanor M. Dorsey, A. Rus Hoelzel and S Jonathan Stern, with the help of many volunteers.

JACKIE O (#4)

This whale was named Jackie O in 1982 because it was photographed so often that year. Jackie was seen repeatedly for several years in San Juan Channel but has not been seen recently. Jackie is covered with small circular scars, many of them obviously old, which suggests that this is an older whale. The fin tilts to the left.

CAPTAIN HOOK (#5)

Captain Hook is named for the hook on the trailing edge of its dorsal fin and is seen almost every summer.   Hook moves all around the San Juan Islands, showing up in all the locations where minkes are seen.

BUBBLES (#7)

Bubbles probaby has the easiest dorsal fin to recognize when seen from the left side because the fin is very pale with a dark horizontal line and a dark tip. In addition, the tip of the fin is bent slightly to the left. Bubbles is named for the big splash it creates when breach-feeding, usually onto its back, and is often seen near Waldron Island.

 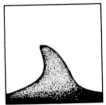

ED (#8)

This whale, a dramatic breach-feeder like Bubbles (#7), is named after Ed Sullivan because it puts on a "really big show." Also like Bubbles, Ed is usually seen near Waldron Island.

181

MINKES WITH DISTINCTIVE FINS

GRANNY SMITH (#9)

This whale has been seen almost every year since 1978, but never frequently and never in a predictable location. Like Jackie O (#4), Granny Smith appears old because of an unusually large number of small circular scars on its body. The fin is bent quite strongly to the left.

TRIBBLES (#10)

Tribbles, named after a creature from Star Trek, has been seen fairly often, usually near Waldron Island.

NIX (#16)

Originally named Nick for a single break in the trailing edge of the fin, this whale had to be renamed in 1984 when the two lower nicks seen here appeared. Nix has been seen almost every year, usually repeatedly, and always south or southwest of San Juan Island.

PANCHO VILLA (#17)

Pancho is seen only occasionally, usually on Salmon Bank off the south end of San Juan Island.

MINKES WITH DISTINCTIVE FINS

TROTSKY (#20)
This whale, named for the sickle-like shape of its fin, has only been seen three times.

FLAPPER (#21)
This whale with a distinctive little flap on the tip of its fin has been seen only once.

POX (#22)
Named for the scallops in its fin, Pox has only been photographed once—on Salmon Bank off the south end of San Juan Island.

CARLOS (#26)
After a long frustrating afternoon with this whale, it was named for an international terrorist who keeps slipping away unphotographed. Carlos is usually seen near Salmon Bank off the south end of San Juan Island. The fin tilts to the left and has an unusually wide base for a minke whale.

183

MINKE FINS/LONG CURVE

STORMY (#1).
Stormy has been seen more often than any other minke whale. Usually Stormy is found south of San Juan Island on either Salmon Bank or Hein Bank. Although its fin is not distinctive, Stormy has a number of small scars that make it quite easy to identify.

QUASIMODO (#3).
This animal is named for the unusual hunched appearance of its spine just in front of the fin. Quasimodo has always been found on Salmon or Hein Bank and is seen almost every year.

LOW RIDER (#6).
Named for its tendency to come to the surface and dive again in such a way that very little of its body is exposed above the water, Low Rider is seen frequently, usually on Salmon Bank off the south end of San Juan Island.

ELECTRA (#11).
This whale has only been seen a few times on Salmon Bank. In spite of the pale color on both sides of its fin, the fin is not considered to be distinctive because the pale color is rather subtle and featureless.

184

MOLE (#12).
Mole has been seen only in one year on Salmon Bank off the south end of San Juan Island.

POSEIDON (#15).
Named for an unusual mark on its left side that looks like a trident, Poseidon is seen quite regularly south of San Juan Island.

GERONIMO (#23).
Geronimo is named after a small pale swath on its left side, which is shaped like a teepee. This whale has been seen only on Salmon Bank.

SUMAC (#27)
This whale has been seen only once, near the Lime Kiln Whale Watch Park on the west side of San Juan Island.

MINKE FINS/SHORT CURVE

BOOKER (#2).
Booker is seen repeatedly each year, usually on Salmon Bank or Hein Bank south of San Juan Island.

WONKILY (#14).
This whale was named for several unusual long depressions on its back and has only been seen once— in 1980.

BEN (#18).
This whale has been seen only three times, always on Salmon Bank off the south end of San Juan Island.

McKINLEY (#19).
McKinley was seen half a dozen times, mostly on Salmon Bank in 1982, but not before or since.

186

TRIANGULAR/MINKE FINS

TROUBLES (#13).
Troubles has been seen most years since 1980, usually near Waldron Island. It is often hard to identify because it has very few scars, and the pale swaths on its sides are almost indiscernable.

HELTER (#24).
Helter and Skelter, whales with almost identical fin profiles, were first seen as a pair swimming very fast away from Salmon Bank off the south end of San Juan Island.

SKELTER (#25).
Skelter has an almost identical fin profile to that of Helter(#24) and has only been seen twice.

HARTWELL (#28).
This whale was seen repeatedly in 1984 on Salmon Bank off the south end of San Juan Island. It appeared to be young because its only circular scars were bright white and obviously new.

CLASSIFICATION

ORDER CETACEA
  Suborder Mysticeti (Baleen Whales)
    Family Balaenopteridae
      Balaenoptera physalus (fin whale)
      Balaenoptera borealis (sei whale)
      Balaenoptera acutorostrata (minke whale)
      Megaptera novaeangliae (humpback whale)
    Family Eschrichtiidae
      Eschrictius robustus (gray whale)
    Family Balaenidae
      Balaena glacialis (right whale)
  Suborder Odontoceti (Toothed Whales)
    Family Kogiidae
      Kogia breviceps (pygmy sperm whale)
    Family Ziphiidae
      Berardius bairdii (Baird's beaked whale)
      Ziphius cavirostris (goosebeak whale)
      Mesoplodon stejnegeri (archbeak whale)
      Mesoplodon carlhubbsi (Hubb's beaked whale)
    Family Phocoenidae
      Phocoenoides dalli (Dall's porpoise)
      Phocoena phocoena (harbor porpoise)
    Family Delphinidae
      Lagenorhynchus obliquidens (Pacific white-sided
        dolphin)
      Delphinus delphis (saddleback dolphin)
      Lissodelphis borealis (northern right-whale
        dolphin)
      Grampus griseus (Risso's dolphin)
      Pseudorca crassidens (false killer whale)
      Globicephala macrorhynchus (pilot whale)
      Orcinus orca (killer whale)
ORDER CARNIVORA
  Family Otariidae (Eared Seals)
    Callorhinus ursinus (northern fur seal)
    Eumetopias jubatus (Steller sea lion)
    Zalophus californianus (California sea lion)
  Family Phocidae (Earless Seals)
    Phoca vitulina (harbor seal)
    Mirounga angustirostris (northern elephant seal)
  Family Mustelidae
    Enhydra lutris (sea otter)
    Lutra canadensis (river otter).

188

FURTHER READING

Angell, Tony and Balcomb, K. C. 1982. *Marine birds and mammals of Puget Sound.* Seattle: Univ. Wash. Press.

Bigg, Michael A.; Ellis, G. M.; Ford, J. K.; and Balcomb, K. C. 1987. *Killer whales of the Pacific Northwest: Their Identification, Genealogy and Natural History.* Vancouver, B. C.: West Coast Whale Research.

Calambokidis, John et al. 1985. *Biology of Puget Sound marine mammals and marine birds.* NOAA Tech. Mem. NOS OMA 18.

Dorsey, Eleanor M. 1983. Exclusive adjoining ranges in individually identified minke whales (*Balaenoptera acutorostrata*) in Washington State. *Canadian Journal of Zoology* 61: 174-181.

Everitt, Robert D.; Fiscus, C. H.; and DeLong, R. L. 1980. *Northern Puget Sound marine mammals.* Springfield, Va.: EPA-600/7-80-139.

Felleman, Fred; Heimlich-Boran, J.R.; Osborne, R.W. 1988 Feeding ecology of the killer whale (*Orcinus orca*). In *Dolphin societies and how we study them.* Pryor, K. and Norris, K.S., eds. Berkeley: Univ. Calif. Press.

Ford, John and Ford, D. 1981. The killer whales of B. C. *Waters* Vol. 5.

Gaskin, David E., 1982. *The ecology of whales and dolphins.* London: Heinemann Educational Books.

Haley, Delphine, ed. 1986. *Marine mammals of eastern North Pacific and arctic waters.* Seattle: Pacific Search Press.

189

Hoyt, Erich. 1984. *The whale watcher's handbook.* Garden City, N. Y.: Doubleday and Company.

___. 1984. *Orca, the whale called killer.* New York: E. P. Dutton.

Jones, Mary Lou; Swartz, S. L.; and Leatherwood, S., eds. 1984. *The gray whale, Eschrichtius robustus.* Orlando, Fla.: Academic Press.

Kirkevold, Barbara and Lockard, J., eds. 1986. *Behavioral biology of killer whales.* New York: A. R. Liss.

Leatherwood, Stephen; Reeves, R. R.; and Foster, L. 1983. *Sierra Club handbook of whales and dolphins.* San Francisco: Sierra Club Books.

Merilees, Bill. 1985. The humpback whales of Georgia Strait. *Waters* Vol. 8.

Minasian, Stanley M.; Balcomb, K. C.; and Foster, L. 1984. *The world's whales.* Washington, D. C.: Smithsonian Books.

Osborne, Richard; Felleman, F.; and Heimlich-Boran, J. 1985. A review of orca natural history. *Cetus* 6:9-11.

Payne, Roger S., ed. 1983. *Communication and behavior of whales.* Boulder, Colo.: Westview Press, Inc.

Pike, Gordon C., and MacAskie, I. 1969. *Marine mammals of British Columbia.* Fish. Res. Board. Can. Bull. 171.

Scheffer, Victor B. 1976. *A natural history of marine mammals.* New York: Charles Scribner's Sons.

Scheffer, Victor B. and Slipp, J. W. 1948. The whales and dolphins of Washington State with a key to the cetaceans of the west coast of North America. *The American Midland Naturalist* 39: 277-337.

Richard Osborne is Research Director of the Whale Museum in Friday Harbor, Washington, a position he has held since 1982. He has worked with captive marine mammals at the old Seattle Marine Aquarium and, in 1976 began field research on local orcas in conjunction with the Moclips Cetological Society. He has also participated in field studies of wild bottlenose dolphins in the Gulf of Mexico and humpback whales in both Hawaii and Alaska.

John Calambokidis is a research biologist with Cascadia Research Collective, a non-profit organization based in Olympia, Washington that specializes in marine mammal research. Since 1976 he has studied marine mammals in Puget Sound and has conducted research on the impacts of pollutants on marine mammals and the biology of harbor seals, northern fur seals, harbor porpoises, gray whales, humpback whales and blue whales in the eastern North Pacific. He has authored numerous technical reports and publications on this research.

Eleanor M. Dorsey is a research associate at the Long Term Research Institute in Lincoln, Massachusetts. Since 1977 she has been involved in studies of the biology and behavior of baleen whales, with emphasis on right whales, bowhead and minke whales, and has published technical papers on these species. In 1980 she began a long-term study of minke whales in the San Juan Islands.

Albert Shepard, a free lance artist based on Orcas Island, Washington, has made his home in the Northwest since 1979. In this region, he has combined a background in the natural sciences and education to render marine mammal drawings and exhibits for the Whale Museum in Friday Harbor, Washington, and to lead sea kayak trips throughout the San Juan Islands.

Ed Newbold is a Seattle-based wildlife artist who works freehand with acrylic paints. His many limited edition prints are available at art fairs in western Washington and at Seattle's Pike Street Market. His artistic goal is to speak for protection of wildlife and the environment, and his financial contributions to these efforts are listed wherever his work is sold.

191